Die (Tooling) Preventive Maintenance for the Sheet Metal Stamping Industry

A comprehensive, step-by-step guide to control your sheet metal stamping process.

Thomas J. Ulrich
Steven E. Ulrich

iUniverse, Inc.
Bloomington

Die Tooling Preventive Maintenance for the Sheet Metal Stamping Industry
A Comprehensive, Step-by-Step Guide to Control Your Sheet Metal Stamping Process

iUniverse books may be ordered through booksellers or by contacting:

iUniverse
1663 Liberty Drive
Bloomington, IN 47403
www.iuniverse.com
1-800-Authors (1-800-288-4677)

ISBN: 978-1-4620-8326-8 (sc)
ISBN: 978-1-4620-8327-5 (e)

Printed in the United States of America

iUniverse rev. date: 3/21/2012

What is Die (Tooling) Preventive Maintenance (PM)?

Using the same tested principles of Equipment PM with:
- Teamwork
- Record Keeping
- Waste reduction
- Communication
- Continuous improvement
-

Planned rehab vs. interrupted production
- Consistent quality
- Continuous production
- Reduced panel storage
- Immediate delivery of product
- Increased profitability

Dedication:

Joe DeOro, my archangel, and
Steven Ulrich, my son and cattle prod

1. Metrology

1.1 Definitions

At the beginning of every chapter I will outline/define all basic concepts and terminology that will be discussed during that chapter. Please refer to these definitions as necessary when reading each chapter, as this will facilitate a better understanding of each concept.

Code Any term, acronym, phrase or symbol utilized as a form of designation for any recordable event.

Dock Audit The last quality-check of stamped parts before they are shipped to the customer.

Die Storage (DS) Die Storage is that floor space which is dedicated to the storage of production tooling in close proximity to its respective maintenance area.

Down Time (DT) Down Time occurs when a press or other manufacturing equipment is idled for any reason. It is no longer producing a salable product.

Fill The amount of salable product that is necessary to: 1) be available to the assembly/finishing operation; 2) provide a similar amount that will, generally, be in transit to the assembly/finishing operation; and, 3) a like amount that is being currently produced.

First Time Capability (FTC) First Time Capability is the ability of a manufacturing process to produce a salable product from the initial (first) cycle of the manufacturing equipment. That is, without any further adjustment.

Just-In-Time (JIT) Just-In-Time production is a system that produces only enough salable product to maintain the "fill" of an assembly process for one day's production.

Last Panel Analysis (LPA) Last Panel Analysis is the inspection of the last panel produced in the stamping process. This inspection should direct the course of activity during the period of time before that tooling is placed in service the next time. (i.e.: storage; steam cleaning; sharpening; repair)

Preventive Maintenance (PM) Preventive Maintenance is a process that provides for regular, scheduled maintenance activities. The particular activities are determined by a particular operation. In general, it means taking the tooling apart and checking components for wear and tear and, then, re-working those components until they are again able to flawlessly perform their primary function. (For purposes of this book, "primary function" means drawing, flanging, forming, lifting, punching, piercing, striking and trimming.)

PM Coordinator The primary responsibility of the PM Coordinator is to market the program and develop it in a logical method consistent with the plant environment and politics. The coordinator must thoroughly understand the process and be committed to the success of die PM. They must also employ the talents and abilities of a management "Champion" to ascertain and develop the methods necessary to ensure success for all concerned.

Recordable Incident (RI) Recordable Incident is a term to describe any occurrence that stops the manufacturing equipment from producing a salable product. Recordable incidents range from a dimpled panel or a missing punch hole to an end-of-run changeover. Legitimate stoppages are recorded as well as those caused by failures of the process itself.

Rework Any activity that is intended to repair or adjust a product to make it salable. Activity includes: burr removal; surface repair; metal finishing; welding; grinding; etc..

Run-to-Run The time from when the last panel of a production run is placed in an appropriate rack for conveyance to the shipping dock or customer to the point when the first panel of the next (different) production run in that press or press line is picked up for placement in an appropriate rack.

Panel Storage (PS) Panel Storage refers to the plant floor space that is occupied by salable product prior to its shipment to its purchasing entity.

Throughput The hourly, shift or daily amount of salable panels produced by any particular manufacturing process. It can be used to evaluate the need for process improvement or to evaluate the effect of a newly implemented process improvement.

Uptime (UT) Uptime refers to the amount of time a production machine is properly operating and available for inclusion in a production process.

1.2 Data Collection

1.2.1 When preparing a case for the implementation of a comprehensive, die-related PM program, the best approach to take is usually the easiest one. Look for the most egregious failures and capture the costs associated with that failure. The problem will be very easily identified. However, do not expect the problem to speak for itself. Prepare the ground by gathering basic facts and figures before anything is done to alter the situation. This is a very important first step. The computer is a tool. It is a tool that stores and sorts information. Use its capabilities to enhance the manufacturing process and record data for process review. The entire program will eventually be measured against the initial datum that is gathered. So… Collecting a lot of different information that relates to various aspects of the particular manufacturing process is a good idea.

1.2.2 The criteria that must be considered are any criteria that affect, or are affected by the condition of tooling being run through a manufacturing process. It may become apparent later that some of the initial datum may not be appropriate and can be discarded. However, surprising as it may be, the most seemingly inconsequential information can take on a new dimension when compared to datum from an improved, in-control manufacturing process. A new participant in the process may have expertise from a different discipline that can utilize such data to identify more obscure failings of the tooling or other steps in the process.

1.3   Customer complaints

1.3.1   For starters, the customer paying the bills should be consulted about their overall product satisfaction.   Of primary importance when consulting the customer are areas where the product does not fulfill customer expectations. Such as inconsistent form, burred edge, missing holes, dirt pimples, liquid deformations, marked panels, etc. Any one or all of the customer complaints can and should be tracked. How many? Per day? Per week? Per month? Severity. Do they stop the process flow? Do they cause time-consuming adjustments to the assembly process? Obviously, there is much to document. And each piece of information needs to be categorized and, possibly, coded for reference and sorting purposes. While this may seem like tedium when being collected, the compiled data can speak loudly in favor of implementing a PM program.

1.3.2   What manager does not enjoy reporting that their customer has realized an actual 25% reduction in manufacturing / product complications? Or, that the end-user saved (x) hours of labor cost because system alterations were not needed? It doesn't matter whether the customer is internal or external to the plant. Before they sign-off on the panels received, before the check is sent, the customer wants what they are paying for or they will let anyone and everyone know about their dissatisfaction. Sounds like a good place to start tracking information.

1.4   Dock Audit

Nomenclature may vary according to specific industry but the term "dock audit" generally refers to the inspection process immediately preceding the shipment of finished panels and or products. It is the final quality check before leaving the plant and should be the spot where every failure is caught. Nice thought, but not 100% foolproof. The most common reason that it is not foolproof is due to the fact that there are so many failures waiting to leave the plant. Logging the type and incidence of panel failures can prove to be a good measure by which to rate the effectiveness of a PM program.

1.5 Downtime

1.5.1   Downtime is this author's favorite measure of manufacturing success, or failure, by far! When presses stop, production stops and costs can, and will, accumulate rapidly. This measure of success or failure is so effective that the introduction of a comprehensive PM program can be justified solely upon the costs and/or savings calculated from measured manufacturing downtime. With a list of simple codes that describe every type of system failure and the willingness to record each incident that causes the process to stop, basic data can be compiled that will give an accurate picture of any manufacturing system's effectiveness.

1.5.2   Downtime Chart (example)

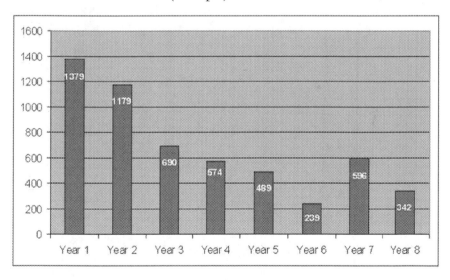

Note: In Year 7, a general foreman took charge in the die room when he came from midnights. Because of his responsibility for the new product launch, he took almost every die maker from PM and used them to support the launch. The PM program suffered immediately and hours increased dramatically. Year 6 was the first year that every die was in the PM program from birth. The results of the fiasco in Year 7 are clear to see during the ensuing years.

1.6   Uptime

1.6.1   Often, the big picture of a comprehensive PM program is not palatable to many managers and the data can be suspect for accuracy. One cannot allow simple social politics to dissuade them from collecting data that are relevant to understanding overall manufacturing effectiveness, whether or not it is data associated with manufacturing downtime or overall end product quality. Natural interaction and an understanding of the importance of the data collected is all that is needed to force the managers and their data recorders to be accurate and fair.

1.6.2   Consider what may happen when, for example, the die room is charged with the previous day's downtime for an automation failure. First, the die supervisor will read the report and see that his area is being charged unfairly. Then, the supervisor walks over to the stamping line and challenges the production supervisor based on the erroneous information that is now part of the general plant production history (and that will now reflect unfavorably on the efforts of the die room). The stream of apologies that will follow is subordinate to the fact that, in the future, whomever is doing the actual recording of information will be a lot more careful about what downtime is charged to which department.

1.7   First-time-capability

1.7.1   Does the line run when it is first set? Many things work against achieving FTC such as, presses, automation, tooling, material control, racking and transportation. All of these considerations directly affect the manufacturing process. All of these considerations also make FTC an opportunity to rate the effectiveness of each aspect of the process. Measures such as this can be combined with a downtime program to achieve an effective measure of reliability.

1.8 Last-panel-analysis

1.8.1   LPA entails an inspection program for every "last" panel off the line before die set. Checking the form and the dimensions of the final panel can give a fairly accurate picture of the condition of the tooling. It can be the impetus for sending the dies to the die room for minor – or major – adjustment. This analysis can keep your process in control by systematically eliminating minor problems that do not necessarily stop the presses but, if left untended, can develop into a process failure that stops production and begins the accumulation of DT. Because downtime is unproductive and costly, die maintenance performed by and in the die room is much easier and affordable since there is no costly press involved that should run at 15+ strokes per minute.

1.9 Rework

1.9.1   Rework generated by an uncontrolled production process is a very significant measure to use since the rework operation requires valuable floor space, skilled personnel, special tools, temporary jigs and fixtures, and special handling. Not to mention that special finishes for the sheet metal will be adulterated. This may not be an on-going measure that is collected every week but it can be effective when compared on a semi-annual basis. The initial dimensions, the manpower, etc. must be collected and stored in a database for referral at the later date. In today's manufacturing environment where cost-justification analysis is regularly applied, constant reminders of program effectiveness are essential to ensure the continued success of die PM and the resultant benefits to the bottom line profits.

1.10 Run-to-Run

1.10.1   The amount of time between when the last panel of a production run is placed in a rack and when the first panel of the next production run is placed in a rack is called Run-to-Run. Achieving world-class run-to-run times is necessary to remain competitive with other manufacturers. The run to run time must be counted in minutes –

not hours – and the minutes should be single digits (under 10 minutes). *Read The SMED System by Shingo*

1.10.2 Measuring the current process is very important before embarking on the implementation of an effective PM program. Knowing exactly what causes increased run-to-run time is essential. Having well maintained and working dies does not help when process automation is causing damage or is mal-forming a panel that will not pass inspection. The more detail the better. (See 1.16)

1.11 Panel Storage

1.11.1   If a plant has not already achieved JIT capability, it has another measure to record before beginning a die PM program. That measure is the plant floor area devoted to panel storage(PS). It is not necessary to survey the plant floor with engineers. Simply stepping off the storage areas will be close enough. The total area occupied by fill panels will be an effective measure to evaluate the reliability of the stamping dies, indeed, the entire stamping process. There is an actual cost, per square foot, of floor space. Most metrics are best reduced to dollars and cents. Everyone understands cost and its relationship to profit.

1.11.2   When the process is not reliable, extra panels must be stored to provide fill. When a manufacturing line is down for inevitable repairs, fill from storage can be sent to the customer so that their production process may continue.   Everyone uses fill panels. Everyone stores racks of panels. The measure will become how many racks, or days, of panels are necessary. The goal should be a twenty-four hour supply. Enough to provide the time necessary to make other arrangements should a catastrophic failure occur.

1.11.3   On the way to achieving a JIT capability, through a comprehensive PM program, more and more floor space will become available. This space can be converted to a productive use. Meaning that this space will provide income as opposed to another space that costs money for upkeep (taxes, heat, lights, etc.). If the PS is properly recorded at the beginning of a PM program, it can provide another indication of program effectiveness and long-term benefit to the entire operation. Too often, managers seek to perpetuate their program to ensure their personal continuous employment. It is much more effective to add to plant profitability and to let the measure speak for itself.

1.12 Throughput

Modified by the word "salable", the simplest measure to use as an indicator of PM success is throughput. How many panels were produced this run? How many were produced last month? Last year? Reliable tooling increases throughput. To prove that premise, current production figures must be captured and recorded for later reference and comparison.

1.13 Uptime

1.13.1 Interestingly enough, the opposite of Downtime is Uptime, the time that your process is operating and producing quality parts. While it can be seen as a positive approach to measurement, it should be used in conjunction with downtime so that failures can be remedied and processes can be improved. Uptime really reflects the reliability of a process. In that context, the simple comparison showing increased uptime will be an effective, albeit general, measure of process reliability.

1.14 Variability

1.14.1 Variability is the bane of any manufacturing process. If presses, automation and tooling are properly maintained and if the sheet metal is of consistent quality and dimension, parts will be cookie-cutter perfect from start to finish and from run to run. If a manufacturing facility does not currently measure variability, it should– if it wants to remain competitive in a world market such as exists today. A comprehensive PM program for dies must improve and become a systematic approach to eliminate variability or something is drastically wrong and the program must be altered. There is no other reason to employ a PM process. Reduction of variability should be the primary goal of a stamping/ assembly plant. As a result, elimination of variability must be a primary measure of die PM effectiveness. FTC, LPA, DA or any other quality

9

check can be used to measure variability as long as they are quantified and accurately reported.

1.15 Codes

1.15.1 Use downtime codes to flag failure. Details can be added to another field of the database or spreadsheet. As it should become more apparent as the program matures, a lot of data are being entered into a computer database. Coding of failures makes it much easier to sort and identify and then initiate corrective actions. Coding also enables easy comparisons to indicate improvements in the process. The details accompanying each failure record allow a comprehensive analysis of recurring problems. The codes allow quick identification of the number of occurrences and re-occurrences of specific failures.

1.15.2 For statistical purposes, incidents of DT should be coded and assigned an accurate amount of lapsed-time. The codes can come from the attached list or they can be custom to a plant. If a custom list is preferred, simply ask the relevant trades people to meet and identify possible causes of failure. After the causes are identified, it should be relatively easy to devise and assign an appropriate three-letter code to each cause. For DT, the codes should be general in nature or the list will become too cumbersome and invite inaccurate entries (because it's too hard to look through a book of possible codes). DT codes should be contained on one or two sheets of paper so they can be taped to a table close to where the data is collected and recorded.

1.15.3 Example of code use

Downtime Accummulation by Die															
Die Number	Assigned Press	Accum Hits	DT Code	January Hours				February				March			
				Wk 1	Wk 2	Wk 3	Wk 4	Wk 1	Wk 2	Wk 3	Wk 4	Wk 1	Wk 2	Wk 3	Wk 4
12345-3	3*2	1022	DBU	1.25											
		1022	MBR		3										
		2044	EWC		1										
		4088	DSS			0.25									
		9198	DFS										1.5		
		9198	DTO										0.5		
		12264	ATV												1

DT Code Use

1.16 Identify Costs

1.16.1   Once a code has been assigned to an incident, the next thing to assign is the elapsed time associated with the failure. The accumulated time will become the most important measure since time can be assigned a dollar value.

1.16.2   Identifying the dollar value of time is a job best left to the Comptroller of the facility. Even though many managers are capable of doing this, credibility demands that a financial person come up with the number. As a class of people, comptrollers have seen every sort of scam and hoodwink known to man. They probably take a class devoted to scams and hoodwinks when they are trained in college. Every proposal that comes to them shows all of the glorious benefits to be received and only a few of the negatives. This may explain their predilection against new, unproven programs.

1.16.3   Ask for a cost per square foot of empty floor space and then ask for the cost of a press line that is standing idle. That is taxes, amortized equipment cost, heat, lights, maintenance and debt service (maybe). Do not ask for costs associated with loss of production such as overtime and panel repair. Do not even ask for the cost of a work crew that may be standing idle while a fix is being made. Just the basic figure is all that is needed. Before long, everyone in the facility will know the value of one hour of press downtime. In fact, because the figure will be unexpectedly high, the cost awareness will prompt most personnel to pay attention to their work environment and join the effort to reduce costs

1.17 Recorder

1.17.1   The person who actually records a failure may not be the person responsible for it being recorded. A line (or floor) supervisor should be held responsible for entering the data into a properly constructed database and it is up to them to assign and train a person to complete the task on a regular basis. There is no need to wait for the Preventive Maintenance (PM) program to begin. Preliminary data collection can provide a base line from which to measure the success of the overall program and it also serves a useful purpose in that issues can be worked out without the pressure that comes with a running responsibility.

1.17.2   To emphasize a previous point, the data collected must be used and disseminated in a report form on a daily basis for it to become and remain accurate. Expect it to be challenged from time to time. Human error or mistakes in judgment will always arise. Responses to the errors will be incremental changes to the collection process that will further enhance the validity of the data.

1.17.3   A DT code and elapsed time should be recorded as soon as a failure occurs during the stamping/production process. Presume that everyone's memory is faulty and insist on immediate entry of the data. If this important step is allowed to become casual, it will probably not be done - let alone be done with any measure of accuracy. Whether the codes are taken from this text or developed by resident trades people, the list should be kept next to the place where the data is recorded so it provides an easy reference.

1.17.4   A computer seems to be the most logical device to handle large amounts of data such as will be generated by a DT program. There are scads of software programs that are geared to maintenance PM. Some of these programs can be customized to run a die PM program. If the budget is small, a database can be designed on software such as MS Access that will facilitate the recording and reporting of DT data. Commercial software has many advantages to its use. But, it is better to proceed with something that is affordable than not to proceed at all. Time and labor costs would dictate that a computer and operator be made available – at least part-time – to handle data entry, storage and retrieval.

1.17.5   For initial analysis purposes, because long-term use of a paper system doesn't seem feasible, hand-written entries can be used to gather base-line information. The assumption is that a PM initiative begs implementation but managers are not aware of the actual magnitude of their problem. Anyone with a pencil, paper, and list of codes can record DT for a designated period of time. Data would then be compiled by hand and included in a report to management detailing the breadth and depth of the die maintenance situation.

1.17.6 Whether by hand or with the help of a computer, collected data can be compiled to, at least, generate interest in a "show me more" program that can lead to a comprehensive PM program. Data are impossible to refute when they are taken without prejudice and presented matter-of-factly in a dollars and cents format. Managers know the language of money and respect those who speak their language. After all, profits equal bonuses and... Who gets paid first?

1.17.7 The initial stage, most likely, will be the "show me more" stage. Even one set of problem dies will quickly prove the efficacy of a PM program. In fact, the worse the die the better candidate it becomes. Solving one problem will earn the right to take on an entire press line of dies, then two, three and more. Eventually, the entire stamping operation will be under a PM program.

Identifying Costs

1.18 Idle Time

1.18.1 It is almost essential to cite idle time as a cost consideration. Is there a manager anywhere who hasn't bemoaned the fact that money is going down the rat-hole whenever they see even one idle worker, let alone an entire work crew. The manner in which most stampers currently operate demands that work crews are floating entities that can leave one line at first sight of a problem and "float" to another line that is already set and cleared for production. The floating concept is directly tied to the fact that the process is unstable. Frequent failures have taught expensive lessons that forbid assigning a crew to a particular production line. They feel that the stamping operation is too tough to fix, so it follows that management must provide additional resources to accomplish the contracted production.

1.18.2 Another "idle time" cost that is often ignored is the cost of a trade person that is assigned to a line for the sole purpose of keeping the line running. It must be easier to pay an extra person to trouble-shoot a constantly failing stamping system than it is to maintain a reliable stamping process. When even the lower volume runs demanded by a weak application of a just-in-time program can't be completed without a stoppage of some sort, it is time to take action. The metric to measure then becomes the cost of the extra personnel who must be employed to service the tooling that is repeatedly failing. As the stamping process improves, there will be less need for "troubleshooters" who cost money. These trade people can be re-assigned to profitable enterprise.

1.18.3 Idle time must be considered down time. However, for the purposes of measurement, it is better to separate the two concepts and reserve down time for interruptions in production when panels are being run. Idle time is regarded as time when either someone or something is not working. An idled work crew or trade person is an obvious loss of productivity when they have no available work to perform. But, the biggest culprit of idle time cost is an inactive press. Downtime ends when a work crew is re-assigned to a production capable line. The considerable cost incurred by a non-operating press line accumulates 24 hours a day and seven days a week. Business assets are on hand to provide manufacturing production, provide cash to cover employee wages, and create larger profits. If a business asset is idle for any reason, the asset does not fulfill its purpose and immediately becomes a business liability. The extra attention paid to the most obvious problems with an idle time tracking process will pay good dividends and provide another fiscally sound reason for implementation and support of an ongoing PM program.

1.19 Re-work

1.19.1 The list of possible reasons for re-working a panel prior to shipping to the customer include: missing holes; burred edges; outboard/inboard flanges; dimples; coin marks; splits; and any number of specialized failures. Scrap can be included here, as well, when establishing a start point for measurement of the PM program's effectiveness. Some problems are particular to skin or exposed panels, and justify added expense, because the cost of manufacturing is greater for these panels due to the fact that their surfaces must be free of defect and pleasing to the eye.

1.19.2 If the representative cost of re-work is to be established, the numbers and types of panels should be recorded monthly and an average cost calculated. Also, look to establish an average tonnage per month measure. After all, if dies are properly cared for and properly handled, what does it matter what panels are run through the production process? Doesn't the buyer specify a good panel? Customers will expect panels within certain specified tolerances. Truth be told, the customers order, need, and require panels that are produced according to the exact specifications of the original design.

1.19.3 For this metric, determine the existing floor space devoted to re-working panels, compute the cost of the personnel doing the work and their supervisors, equipment, perishables, hand tools, etc. These data and the scrap information provide another opportunity for evaluating the PM process. Return to the calculations for Panel Storage (1.11.1). measure the area used by the re-work team to fix panels, add the cost of the personnel, etc. (above) and include the cost of extra parts containers as well as the floor space used to store them while the individual parts are being repaired and the entire cost of re-work will be captured.

1.19.4 Need a formula? Try:

Work Floor Space x Square foot burden   1000 x 1.20 = 1200.00
+ ({num. of emps) x (Emplymt exp.)}   8 x 200.00 x 20= 32000.00
+ Average Monthly Supply cost   1000.00
= Storage Floor Space x Square Foot Burden 1500 x 1.20 = 1800.00

= Total Cost of Re-work per month   36000.00
These numbers are hypothetical and conservative but can be obtained from any plant comptroller. As with every metric, determine a present day starting point so that there will be an accurate point of deviation to illustrate the effectiveness of the ongoing PM initiative.

1.19.5 Possibly an example will help to see the possible ramifications of a properly controlled stamping program. When this author began his life as a PM Coordinator, the plant allocated a sizable area of the plant to reworking panels. There were six (6) OBI presses and a small gap frame press to re-stamp panels for re-strike purposes and some were used to add missing holes. A hi-lo and driver were assigned to the area as well as small hand-operated pallet lifters, hand trucks, etc.. Cabinets for tools and personal safety equipment took up a bit of room as well. Generally, there were 30+ people working in the area (expanded as needed) and the area was contained within an 80 ft. bay that was over 100 feet in length. After five (5) years of die PM and related process improvements, the area housed tool boxes and workbenches for five people per shift x two shifts with no ancillary equipment save metal finishing files and hand tools. Even that reduction in expensive re-work is not enough. But, that giant reduction is a measure of success by which the PM program is measured.

1.19.6   This example is given and this story is told because every shop has things that are taken for granted (i.e.: "necessary evils"). These failures, though, must be the target of an overall commitment to process improvement and to die preventive maintenance in particular.

1.20 Inventory storage space

1.20.1   Earlier in this text, the cost of empty floor space was mentioned as well as what criteria to use when assigning a value to it. This measure is where that value is assigned. The author would walk off the area and call it good enough. Whatever your method, determine the effective floor space devoted to the storage of panels. Include floor space used by all parts storage containers: open and closed boxes; mesh containers; dunnage racks; small lot containers; anything with a part in it. There is a valid reason why larger volume "partner" customers are concerned about storage needs and the associated cost. Storage does cost money and it invariably adds to the price of the product being manufactured.

1.20.2   If the number one customer is aware of the cost of storage space, then measurement and evaluation of that space becomes a necessity.   Space required to facilitate production purposes and shipping needs are perfectly acceptable and expected to be included in the manufactured product. Storage of several days of production to provide leeway when dies are out of service due to poor maintenance practices is a convenience for the manufacturer and, by rights, should not be passed on to the customer. When this principle is accepted and the financial burden of storage space is shifted to plant costs, there may be a different attitude toward support of the costs of space. Especially when that space can be converted to value-added activities that provide profit for the shareholders.

1.20.3 Invariably, as the resident tooling deteriorates, production increases and capacity decreases. More and more of the existing floor space is given up to the storage of over-production. Interesting thing to note is that, somehow, the need for more storage space stops when storage capacity is filled. With nowhere else to go, management will, finally, implement measures to keep the process under "control". Unfortunately, few managers pay attention to the losses incurred when floor space is misused. Failure could be expressed in terms of unproductive floor space. Try this exercise:

> Amass the actual cost of the property by adding yearly taxes to annualized building cost and general (janitorial-type) maintenance expense;
> Figure the cost per square foot;
> Pace off the area that encompasses the production lines;
> Figure the revenue received from that profit-center;
> Calculate the revenue per square foot for your production lines;
> Pace off the area currently used for storage of panels;
> Figure the annualized cost per square foot (use figure from line 2 to calculate);
> Subtract line 7 from line 5;
> Multiply line 8 x square footage of current storage area (line 6);
> The answer (line 9) reveals how much is at stake.

1.20.4 Converting unproductive space to productive floor space is a wonderful gauge when used to evaluate a die PM program. Improvement is sometimes subtle and incremental. That is why it is important to gather this basic data prior to implementation of the program. Preparing a folder on the computer's hard drive for "Improvement Measures" will prove to be a very rewarding exercise.

1.20.5 All roads lead back to the Controller. Floor space, again, is best valued in a minimalist fashion. Amortized construction cost + taxes + utility expenses allocated to heat and general lighting + water and sewerage = cost of having an unproductive floor available. When evaluating productive space, take the total square footage of all the production areas and divide that number into the total sales volume of panels sold. Every area can be valued separately, of course, but a general average should suffice for comparison purposes. Details are needed in sufficient number to provide credibility to the basic values used for comparison, but averages based on the details are usually sufficient when constructing charts and reports that show the progress attained by a die PM program

1.21 Manpower

1.21.1 For this metric, count the number of employees directly employed by the production operation. Count them by trade and classification. Count the supervisors and their support personnel on salary. Count those who are forced to handle the storage requirements and count those who do re-work of the panels. Finally, count those who feed the scrapped panels into the baler. This will be a slow-moving list to track but, when compared at six month intervals, it can be a very effective promotional device to help solidify support for die PM among plant staff.

1.21.2 Every person employed at a manufacturing facility is considered an asset and is expected to provide some measure of value (monetary or otherwise) to the manufacturing activity. If production and material handling employees are forced to wait for tools and dies to be repaired instead of running production, their time and their cost is considered wasted. It is an easy concept to understand. Too much waste = no profit = no paycheck.

1.21.2 It may seem that a comprehensive PM program for dies would result in fewer employees being needed. In this author's experience, working in a union represented stamping facility, recorded numbers of employees actually increased after the implementation of a comprehensive PM program. For example, the transition to full PM implementation, since 211 die makers could not keep 28 failure-plagued major press lines working with any regularity, required 50 extra die makers for transitional support of the dies that filled these 28 lines.

Seven years later, 110 die makers accomplished what 211 could not — they kept the production lines running without interruption specifically caused by tooling failures. Presently, 140 die makers are used for construction of new dies (a new profit center) and to support the 30 new sub-assembly lines. Increased reliability allowed use of modern transfer presses and subsequent re-assignment of production workers to these new sub-assembly areas. These areas were made possible by vacated storage space. By attrition, skilled supervision decreased from 28 to 6 in the die maintenance area. That reduction was the only negative associated with PM. There was a real increase in employment at this facility directly related to a comprehensive PM plan.

1.21.4 Why pay a trade person to baby-sit a production line? Why not work to ensure that production runs from start to finish without interruption? Ace trade persons work much better when they are not constrained by time and material. Time to affect a proper repair of a small problem is much better than applying a band-aid on a problem that will only grow more acute because hurried repairs are partial repairs. Unprepared for the failure, oft times, materials are substituted in a short-term fix - further exacerbating the problem.

1.21.5 Die PM is a deliberate program that gradually changes the work environment. Because it is a slowly developing process, changes are incremental. Luckily, the changes are also dramatic and, therefore, supportive of the on-going PM effort. Cutting the number of die makers assigned to production support in half should be a primary goal of a PM program. Because the changes are slow, reassignment to a more productive endeavor is possible in a measured fashion. Skilled trades people are too valuable to send on their way. Use their skills and experience to enhance plant profitability. They can populate a new die construction initiative (in an area made possible by reducing panel storage). They can, alternatively, maintain dies used in a new production area. New products; new production areas; sub-assembly lines: all are possible after the process is brought under control via a comprehensive die PM program.

1.22 Employee Morale Indicators

1.22.1 Attitude, attitude, attitude are the three principles by which employee morale is measured. The main point is that the employees measure management's attitude more than management measures the employees' attitude. They do not listen to what management says as much as they look at what management does. An oral commitment to safety must be backed with an actual attempt to remove unsafe conditions in the workplace. For example, when management demands a quality product and endorses quality with a pro-active program such as die PM, employees climb onto the bandwagon and look for ways to help improve not only the product but also the process. It's human nature, plain and simple. They are going to be working for an 8-hour shift and they would rather make good parts than make rejects. They definitely don't want to go home and tell the family that they made 8,145 rejects today.

1.22.2 To better measure the benefits attached to management's commitment to quality and productivity, the average number of safety violations recorded per month should be recorded and placed in the "Improvement Measures" folder. The same should be done with employee grievances (if they are collected), the number in an absentee correction process, the number of suggestions received per month and, finally, the number of employees seeking a promotion. All are indicators of employee morale that can be used as a measure of improvement after implementing a comprehensive die PM program.

1.23 Compiling a Current State Report/ Analysis

1.23.1 After all the foregoing data has been gathered, it is time to prepare a Current State Report. Maybe all the data will be shared at the outset. Maybe very little will be used. The plant politics and the best judgement of the PM Coordinator will determine what is shared and what is held back for a later time. The point is that all the preliminary data should be formatted and included in a report that details the location of the basic information (the "Improvement Measures" folder) as well as outlining the standard by which improvements will be gauged.

See "Current State Report Example" in Appendix.

1.23.2 The aforementioned table lists the various reports that should have value when promoting the installation or continuation of a comprehensive PM program. The "When" column indicates when the data should be collected, not necessarily when they are charted and presented. The PM Coordinator's discretion should govern when sufficient change has occurred to make the different reports meaningful and indicative of significant improvement resulting from the PM program.

1.23.4 Recipients: when produced, charts and all reporting mechanisms should be presented to all members of the management staff. Each staff person should get their own copy and a copy should be posted in the room where daily meetings are held. Each supervisor should get copies of charts that are pertinent to their area of responsibility. Typed "general status" reports should be prepared whenever there is a change in the staff roster, in addition to the regular semi-annual reporting schedule. The important consideration is that reports be regular and brutally accurate, even when the results are less then positive. Honesty should be rewarded with credibility.

1.23.5 Occasionally, situations will occur that demand immediate attention. A Special Report will highlight these situations. One instance, in this author's experience, provides a good example. In Year 0, the first of a continuing installation of modern, hi-tech transfer presses was accomplished. A particular crew of production workers and skilled tradespeople, along with a supervisor, were specially trained by the manufacturer and installed along with the press. They were a Team and, generally, made collective decisions about how they would operate. Management allowed this and supported them as long as production quotas were attained. When asked to consider including their new dies in the PM program, the work crew declined the offer. This team felt that they could maintain their own new dies with their own "system". In Year 4, their dies were the only dies in the plant that were not included in the die PM program. This crew was experiencing problems keeping up with die sets and die maintenance – all the while insisting that their process was working but they were understaffed.

1.23.6 The author researched the situation, collected the relative die downtime data and compared it to the average die downtime experienced by the other production areas in the plant. The special report that was issued showed how this production area was considerably higher than that average (the average included transfer presses, tandem presses and older conventional press lines). Even though the crew called foul and insisted that data *they recorded* were not accurate, the plant manager ordered their inclusion in die PM. The regular maintenance areas were asked to help bring the dies up to standard, prepare blueprint booklets, and design PM check sheets. Even though they continued to insist that there was no need for the PM program, the numbers showed otherwise. Finally, after seven months of inclusion in the PM program, their average downtime fell below the plant average – and stayed there! They also stopped ranting and raving and, grudgingly, conceded that die PM worked. This example shows that when a steady flow of reports and charts is maintained throughout the implementation process, a special report can be used to point the finger at a problem that needs fixing. The reports then become an incentive for collective compliance by the entire shop.

1.23.7 Sales! Without a doubt, the PM Coordinator is a sales person. Even as the PM program matures and pays huge dividends, there will be attempts to discount the program's effectiveness in favor of good, old-fashioned die making. For this reason, the data collected and stored in the Improvement Measures folder will have to be dusted off and used to compile a new report that compares the present success to previous failures. There is a reason why regular communication with Staff and the workforce is critical. Results may be obvious but they must be highlighted and presented to all concerned so that they are reminded of the original conditions which are the catalyst for adoption of a comprehensive Die PM program. This may sound a little like one is conducting a war. In a way, it is just that. Old habits die hard. Past practice always will find defenders who do not want to change the system that they find comfortable. These die-hards forget that their company must continually improve to remain competitive in the world market. Recorded history and simple charts will be effective ammunition to reaffirm the plant wide reliance on PM to lead the continuous improvement initiative.

1.23.8 Another good example: in Year 7 (see chart) a new product introduction occurred. Problems were such that a newly assigned manager decided that PM could be ignored and those die makers assigned to get the new dies ready for launch. Almost immediately, the downward trend of die failures stopped and die-related downtime began to rise. Fast-talking and the urgency of the new launch allowed the situation to continue for several months. In fact, the die-related downtime doubled plant-wide. This abandonment of PM was finally halted when the die-related downtime bar chart was updated to show the average DT hours for those months when PM was ignored. The plant manager did not ignore that chart and the die makers were ordered back to the maintenance shop to continue the care of the stamping dies. The damage to the unattended dies was such that they were not able to gain the same low level of downtime that had been previously achieved. Apparently, preventing damage is much more effective than repairing damage. Another ringing endorsement of die PM!

2.0 – Methodology

2.1 Definitions

Before proceeding, it is necessary to identify the three basic maintenance systems that are currently in use by the manufacturing industries. They are reactive maintenance, preventive maintenance and predictive maintenance. In addition to these three types of maintenance, all basic concepts and terminology that will be discussed during this chapter are defined below. Please refer to these definitions as necessary when reading this chapter, as this will facilitate a better understanding of each concept.

Reactive Maintenance   Reactive maintenance is a very common term, and can be referred to as "fire fighting". This approach to die maintenance is excessively expensive. It fixes the individual component whenever it fails. Weld. Sharpen. Replace. There is a price to pay with downtime, scrap panels and lost production.

Preventive Maintenance   Preventive maintenance (PM) is a process that provides for regular, scheduled maintenance activities. What happens is determined by a particular operation. In general, it means to take the tooling apart and check for wear and tear and then working the components until they are again able to perform their primary function. (For purposes of this book, "primary function" means drawing, flanging, forming, lifting, punching, piercing, striking and trimming.)

Predictive Maintenance   Predictive maintenance (PdM) for tooling is on the way but it has not arrived yet. Basically, PdM is only possible with the assist of electronic technology. The technology should measure wear or breakage and alarm the user when action is required to prevent the manufactured product from being out of the required specification. There are few applications that provide the sensitivity required to do this important job.

Total Productive Maintenance TPM is a process that seeks to eliminate unnecessary maintenance activities while using procedures that deliver just-in-time capabilities through use of a trained, involved, and empowered work force assisted by the robust control of available equipment. Not easy to achieve. Impossible to achieve without a decent PM program and will be considerably easier with a robust PdM technology.

PM Champion A Champion will be a shift superintendent or a manager at the plant staff level. This person will have the ability and inclination to set performance goals and standards for the supervisors under their authority. They will be responsible for designing meaningful reports and identifying the appropriate metrics by which the PM initiative will be measured.

PM Coordinator The primary responsibility of the PM Coordinator is to market the program and develop it in a logical method consistent with the plant environment and politics. The coordinator must thoroughly understand the process and be committed to the success of die PM. They must also employ the talents and abilities of a management "Champion" to ascertain and develop the methods necessary to ensure success for all concerned

Workforce Steering Committee The Workforce Steering Committee is charged with guiding the PM implementation process from the plant floor. They will meet to add or subtract from the existing list of DT codes and repair codes. This committee will help gain support for the program among their fellow workers. If the members represent a variety of disciplines, there will soon be interactions between their respective departments which will use the data and procedures to further their own ends.

2.2 Primary Focus

2.2.1 This book will primarily concern itself with preventive maintenance since PdM and TPM are impossible without a solid basis in PM. The process for implementation should be relatively straightforward. However, politics is a vicious animal and, depending on the culture, extreme care must be taken to avoid destructive confrontations that can stop the initiative dead in its tracks. Based purely on common sense and easily understood, PM tends to make "the way we've always done it" look like a fool's enterprise. Depending on how highly placed the proponents of the status quo are, it is also common sense to temper the implementation of PM with caution, training, and regard for the egos of all concerned.

2.3   Important Elements

2.3.1   When laying the groundwork for implementing a comprehensive tooling PM program, certain important elements must be considered. These elements are critical to the success of the program and should be addressed with care and an understanding of the culture of the facility within which the process will operate. It is important to note that the process should not be delayed until the "just exactly right" person or method is discovered. It is more important to move forward with an eye towards improving the process as it matures and gathers its own legs.

2.3.2   The most important elements are: a suitable champion and an adequate computer system that can carry the data generated by the workforce and the stamping process. These two elements are also mutually supportive in that the champion will frequently make use of the collected data to support the efforts of the PM initiative while the data collection process must be supported by the clout of the champion to ensure that it is accurate and entire in its scope.

2.3.3   A permanent Steering Committee should be formed from among the skilled and production workforces. They can help ascertain the methods of data collection, code generation, training requirements, etc. This committee will, in fact, provide the means to garner support from the hourly employees as an expression, by management, of the value ascribed to workforce involvement in the upcoming culture change. Identifying the manpower need and then hiring transitional manpower– another important element– will also further enhance employee perception of PM as a cultural change that is fully supported and endorsed by their management team.

2.3.4   Oftentimes, the importance of the floor supervisor as a change agent is overlooked. They are an essential element that is necessary to the success of the PM initiative. They must be convinced of management's commitment to the full implementation of a tooling PM program since they will, most likely, assign their workers to collect the data and perform the PM activities contained on the PM checklists. Supervisors are also the primary source of process data against which any improvement must be measured.

2.3.5   Devising a maintenance schedule is a relatively easy, but necessary, process. Providing a rudimentary schedule serves to make the process manageable and understandable to those who perform the activities. It is important to emphasize the fact that the schedule depends on the performance of each particular tool and is, therefore, subject to change.

2.3.6   Every manufacturer is aware that training is an essential aspect of plant life. For the PM program, it is necessary to train or to explain. Depending on the plant culture, it may be necessary to provide a full training program that can identify the benefits associated with a comprehensive PM program (greater productivity, improved quality, more jobs, etc) as well as the expected participation of all levels of the workforce and management. Training also allows a discussion relative to individual responsibilities and methods for improving the PM process as it matures. In other cultures, a simple explanation regarding management-imposed plant goals may suffice.

2.3.7   Floor space is a resource that requires careful consideration. As an element of PM, it is important to allocate sufficient space to allow tear-downs during the checklist activities. These workspaces must also be located near the storage areas that hold the tooling between production runs. Access to, and handling of, the tooling is an important consideration from the aspect of time. Close and available means more time doing quality- based repairs and PM checklist activities. In addition, it is crucial that there be a close proximity to set-up plates and machine tools. They are used on a daily basis to effect repairs to critical elements of each tool. Comprehensive lists of such tools should be researched prior to full implementation of PM. *Another job for the Steering Committee.*

2.4 Champion

2.4.1   When it comes to selecting a Champion, look high. The Champion must command respect and have the ability to determine whether managers and supervisors will continue their employ under this new way of life in the stamping shop. A perfect Champion will be a shift superintendent or a stamping manager or a tooling superintendent, etc.

2.4.2   This Champion must also be able to gain the cooperation of the other department heads as well as members of Plant Staff. Having allies on Staff will enable the Champion to plan and negotiate for such things as added manpower (Human Resource Manager), technological resources (computers, software, electronic measurement devices, etc.), financial data (Comptroller) and production related data (Production Manager).

2.4.3   Of course, having such a high-profile Champion indicates the level of commitment of the Plant Manager/Owner. That important support, when augmented with frequent reports about the increased effectiveness of die PM, will be vital to ensuring the enthusiastic support of trades people, the production crew and their supervisors. It is no secret that members of the workforce in general will wait to see the quantity and quality of committed resources before embracing any management initiative.

2.5 Computer

2.5.1   Next comes the computer, another vital element to consider at program set-up. There are several approaches to consider but, the primary consideration is the database engine. As the PM program develops, it will become necessary to transfer data from old system to new. The ultimate success of any PM program depends on the utilization of stored data. Therefore, selecting a proper database system becomes all-important. dB XX is a standard that many software applications utilize.

MSAccess is a software industry standard. If your system will be PC-based, use one of these. If sufficient resources are available, a custom application can be designed for use on a mainframe. If a mainframe is considered, database storage techniques suitable for a mainframe will be used but, try to retain a familiar screen by using MSAccess as the front end graphic user interface(GUI). Most employees will own home computers and use MS Windows as an operating system. If the same GUI is used as an input device, they will be more familiar with it and, thus, more comfortable using it – increasing use and keeping errors at a minimum. If the plant is small to medium-sized, the local college of engineering may be willing to send a student who is familiar with computers and has a background in mechanical engineering. Paying them to design the forms and working elements of the database will be money well spent and could endear the company to the college administration. However, easy acquiescence to their suggestions is a mistake, the "experts" work in the plant and when it comes to the business, the "consultant" needs direction from the "experts". Finally, don't forget to ask your customer if your customer is a major manufacturer who uses your sub-contracted part in their final product. They just might have their own developed software package.

2.5.2   Design of the database should be approached with caution. Perhaps a simple database can be set up in MSAccess and then adjusted to meet the ever-expanding needs of the developing PM program. Each stamping/production facility has different customs and procedures, or different concerns relative to productivity and tool maintenance. So, starting with basic forms (from this book) a custom system can be designed "on the run" as the needs present themselves and become apparent. Over a period of time, confidence will build relative to database design and what fields may be needed to properly record information necessary to evaluate the die PM process. Software applications that are designed based on experience will certainly be more useful than a "canned" approach – keeping in mind, though, that the "can" may be opened and customized.

2.5.3   The computer person should not add in "neat stuff" like pop-up windows and drop-down menus. Pop-ups and drop-downs tend to confuse the inexperienced user. They also lengthen the time needed to enter simple data. In this author's experience, when computers were installed in every repair/maintenance area as well as in the production areas, trades people had little patience with cumbersome data-entry procedures. Four to five attempts, by trade people, to implement direct data-entry was met with failure. One-page data-entry screens are best – by far.

2.5.4   As data accumulates and confidence builds in its accuracy, more and more interest will be shown in sharing the data between departments. The need for networking will become obvious. By the time that this point arrives, the "design" phase should be complete and written procedures should be implemented to control how data is entered into the database and by whom that data is entered. Access (review only) to the stored data is not as important to control, as is making sure that the data is accurately recorded.

2.5.5   When implementing the PM program, special attention should be paid to the quality and quantity of the data being recorded in the database. Don't make a mistake by selecting only the "important" maintenance incidents. Gather as much data as possible and as many incidents as do occur. Quality refers to coverage, or completeness, of the gathered information. Quantity refers to the brevity or conciseness of the details. Full descriptions of maintenance issues can be most briefly indicated through use of codes. Codes will be explained later in this chapter. For now, suffice to say that meaningful data, properly presented, can be used by anyone to address any relevant matter concerning the efficiency and effectiveness of the in-house stamping process. Guarding data only serves to protect failure and prevent a timely solution of problems.

2.6   PM Coordinator

2.6.1   Equal in importance to the selection of the Champion is choosing an appropriate PM Coordinator. The first choice should be someone who is familiar with the tooling and knows how to repair it. Someone who is also familiar with the capabilities of a computer and can lay out forms, design charts, and compose meaningful reports. Familiarity with MS Office Pro© is a good basic prerequisite for a likely candidate. Obviously, a trade person would be ideal. Start with only one or two individuals who will work closely with the Champion to drive the PM process in the right direction, establishing procedures, designing documents, entering data, etc.

2.6.2   The PM Coordinator(s) will assume leadership of the Skilled Steering Committee and be responsible for identifying proper PM activities for each tool. They should not be responsible to any supervisor – only to the Champion. - Supervisors are more concerned with their own areas of responsibility and could readily prostitute the program to their own perceived benefit. It will be hard enough to keep the process honest without making the Coordinators answer to a floor supervisor. By removing two steps in the chain of command – supervisor and general foreman – the Coordinator has the ability to communicate directly with those who have the greatest responsibility for the efficient and effective operation of the facility. They should deliver, by hand or e-mail, all reports, charts, suggestions and studies to the Champion and concurrently send a copy (CC:) to all members of Staff. Many who firmly believe in the principles of "chain of command" may find this anathema but, assuredly, it is a vital concession to the effectiveness and viability of an on-going PM program. When composing these reports, the Coordinator can be expected to make the recipients aware of program success and failures, wants and needs, and newly formulated goals and objectives.

2.6.3   Friendships can be a problem. It is impossible to prevent working relationships from become fast friendships. (This is not an indictment against forming good working relationships within the plant.) Occasionally, an area's shortcomings may be hidden and statistics falsified due to a wrong-headed sense of allegiance. The only safety measure to regulate this type of abuse is a periodic audit of the database performed by the Comptroller's office/staff. Underlying documentation should be compared to reported results and charts. This is not an entirely negative process. The audit can uncover program inefficiencies and misdirected efforts, opportunities to change purchase procedures for certain supplies, and opportunities to improve tooling design by eliminating failure before it is designed into the tooling (without complaints, in-house design staff tend to resurrect previous designs and change the part-related aspects of the tooling while leaving many, possibly faulty, elements in place). Audits are discovery devices and should be considered an essential part of any program.

2.6.4   A simple table can be computer-designed on MS Excel© to schedule periodic PM activities. Every tool in the facility should have a place on the schedule. The time to develop such a document is now. Using an Excel© (or similar) spreadsheet, list dies, by number, along the "A" column. Across the top row, number the columns from 1 to 52. Using the production schedule, the entire maintenance year can be plotted. For example; die 12345.xx is included in the PM process on 1/1/XX; it produces 5,000 parts a week to meet customer requirements; March 15th should be the scheduled date of PM for that die if it is on a 50k schedule. Assign each set of dies to work teams. Stagger the schedule so that only one die is serviced each day by each team and, eureka, your company now employs a die PM schedule.

2.6.5   Once dies are scheduled and there is visible assurance that the system will work, it is time to prepare a working document to serve as a visible reminder that PM dates are approaching and whether or not a PM has been accomplished on any particular tool. The information that is provided by this working schedule will prove invaluable to the trade person and supervisor alike. This sample shows shading to indicate a completed procedure, italics to show the projected date for the upcoming PM.

Part Number	Die Number	Home Line	Die Supervisor	50K	100K	150K	200K	250K
12345678	D1-23	1	Smith	1/19/2010	2/21/2010	3/9/2010	4/19/2010	*6/1/2010*
	D2-34	1	Smith	1/19/2010	2/21/2010	3/9/2010	4/19/2010	*6/1/2010*
256342	D3-45	1	Smith	1/19/2010	2/21/2010	3/9/2010	4/19/2010	*6/1/2010*
Latest prod. count	D4-56	1	Smith	1/19/2010	2/21/2010	3/9/2010	4/19/2010	*6/1/2010*
23456789	D1-23	2	Jones	2/9/2010	02/29/2010	4/30/2010	*6/1/2010*	
	D2-34	2	Jones	2/9/2010	02/29/2010	4/30/2010	*6/1/2010*	
226451	D3-45	2	Jones	2/9/2010	02/29/2010	4/30/2010	*6/1/2010*	
Latest prod. count	D4-56	2	Jones	2/9/2010	02/29/2010	4/30/2010	*6/1/2010*	

PM Schedule Example

2.6.6   Software is available to handle most aspects of scheduling PM activities. The main point to remember, though, is that the PM process can begin whether or not fancy software is available. Software does not make the PM process successful, getting the work done does.

2.7 Failure Codes

2.7.1   Before downtime monitoring begins, an experienced group of workers from every department of the plant should meet to brainstorm possible failures. These are incidents of failure that may occur during a production run. It is best to not get complicated. A three-letter code is sufficient. Coded entries are easier to sort in a database. It also makes data easier to analyze. Mainly, knowing what failed, when it failed and how long the presses were stopped is all that is needed. By using a coded entry, the operator can quickly enter the hour, the code and the elapsed time directly into a computer terminal or into a back-pocket notebook for later entry into a database. As the process comes under control, the need for more detailed information will become apparent. Again, a simple code is best. Try Exx for electrical failure; or Dxx for a die failure; or Axx for automation; and so forth.

See "Suggested Downtime Codes Example" in Appendix

2.7.2   While on the subject of codes, the coordinator should consider using work-specific teams to develop a series of codes that describe the actual causes of failure. These codes are much more specific than failure (downtime) codes because these are used by the crafts when they have taken the die (press, motor, etc.) apart and examined the components. The entire code should have three numeric fields and two alpha-numeric fields to contain the information.

2.7.3   The craft person will, after inspection, know the actual cause. That cause should be entered in the database. Everything mentioned before about what makes the failure codes valuable and easy to analyze still applies: coded entry makes analysis easier. Adding a location (alpha-numeric) code should also be considered. It will enable one to track repair durability and effectiveness. Was it really welded properly? Is ion-nitriding worth the expense? Does the weld rod live up to the promised quality? Are these answers worth knowing? With careful planning and accurate collection of specific data, those answers will be available down the road – when there is the time and need for close analysis.

2.7.4   This series of codes should be numeric to distinguish them from the alpha failure codes. Obviously, operators and craft people are the best candidates to determine the appropriate coded entries.

2.8   Checklist Development

2.8.1   The process to determine each individual activity that must appear on any particular PM checklist is a lengthy one. Experience is a key element. Visual evaluation takes time, too much time when hundreds of tools are being entered into the plant PM program. Therefore, it is best to use a generic form – generic for each type of tool. Reproducing this form will be the easiest method to use when initiating the PM process. This is a sample of a checklist that might be used for draw dies:

See "Draw/Redraw PM Checklist" in Appendix

2.8.2   By encouraging the workforce to comment and edit the form, the PM Coordinators can arrive at an accurate description of each particular tool and build that description on a form that is unique to each tool. This is especially important in this day when tooling is designed to perform many functions, (i.e.: draw dies that lance/pierce; pierce dies that flange; etc.). The MS Excel Workbook© is an excellent device to use when storing checklists for multiple tools used to produce one part. Bear in mind that each tool in a "family" of dies will be reaching the cycle-frequency PM level at the same time and all the appropriate checklists can be printed easily by selecting "Print" and then "Entire workbook".

2.8.3   Some procedures that must be followed are common tasks that are appropriate for each and every tool. It is a relatively simple task to add, on the back of each checklist, a list of procedures to follow each time the tool is released back to production after completing a scheduled PM. The list could look like the following:

See "Standard Operating Procedure Example" in Appendix

Or it can be altered to meet the needs of a particular die, much the same as the PM checklist. Obviously, a computer printer with duplexing capabilities is best designed for this purpose.

2.9 Communication

2.9.1   Communication is vital to the success of any manufacturing process. The stamping of sheet metal is no exception. The physical well-being of tooling is best served by immediate resolution to any and all failures that occur during the stamping process. Dull trim steels may not be as important as a malfunctioning transfer bar but, given time, it can stop the production run just as surely as a smashed transfer bar. Repairing the problem, obviously, requires an order of priorities. A priority can be established based on severity, location, panel type, ease of repair, availability of material to repair the problem and critical need of product to ship to the customer. When the alarm bell is rung, who will show up to survey the damage? There is no need for an army of "consultants" to offer opinions on the breadth and depth and importance of the failure. A die maker is all that is needed to sharpen a trim edge. The plant head of purchasing may be needed to assist with a damaged transfer bar, whether they are at home in bed, at lunch, or at their desk.

2.9.2   To assemble the proper damage-control team, it may be wise to employ a list of codes that can accurately describe the "severity, location, panel type, ease of repair, availability of material to repair the problem and critical need of product to ship to the customer". Each aspect can be identified as one or two digits and, when strung together, easily transmitted to pre-determined personnel via PDA or other communication device. Many computer software programs are available that will send pages to a list of recipients automatically. The recipients can then determine their own level of interest/involvement before journeying to the crash site. Additionally, the page is received simultaneously by all recipients and that saves time. A code will also avoid miscommunication and misunderstanding due to factory noise and second-hand information.

2.9.3   The use of a computer is almost a necessity when implementing and developing a comprehensive PM program for tooling. It is a storage device. It is a communicator. It is an evaluator. It is not a brain. It cannot gather information without input. It cannot determine the validity of any data that is entered into its disk storage device. The plant PM program requires an adequate, up-to-date computer as much as it requires a pro-active, participating Champion, a skilled, dedicated PM Coordinator(s) and a professional workforce.

2.10 Workforce Steering Committee

2.10.1   The most important element in the PM process is the skilled workforce. They are where "the rubber meets the road". In the current manufacturing climate, which seeks to emulate the Japanese approach, they are the subject matter experts when seeking to improve a process. This is absolutely true for tooling PM and these skilled workers should be used to advantage when identifying codes, procedures, equipment, and developing checklists.

2.10.2   The Workforce Steering Committee (WSC) should be chaired by the PM Coordinator. Their assigned task should always be to improve their work environment based on principles of safety and quality, with efficiency thrown in for good measure. The line troubleshooter should be represented in the committee membership as well as the repair die maker. Possibly, a supervisor can be included as long as they do not hold sway and have an unbalanced influence on the outcome. If there are new-construction die makers, or a try-out team on hand, they should be represented too. There is no need to overstaff the WSC. Four or five trade people are sufficient to meet the needs of the developing program.

2.10.3   Each WSC (from maintenance, tooling, assembly, quality, etc.) should, at the outset, brainstorm a list of possible failures that can occur during the operation of their particular process. Lists in hand, representatives from each WSC should then meet to determine the final make-up of the list of failure codes. Seemingly similar problems have to be identified and defined so that there is no misunderstanding relative to which area of operation is responsible for effecting a return to service on the production line. The following, combined list is provided as a guide. Each facility has its own language and unique production system. It is important that every department has a list of failure codes for their particular area of responsibility. There is no need to have a code for each itemized problem. Rather, failure codes should be general in nature since they will work best in tandem with a complete set of more specific root cause codes. The codes must be general and simple enough for anyone to use. Many times, the one who ascribes the failure code may be a production person or a clerk – one who has no technical expertise.

2.10.4

See "Downtime Codes Example" in Appendix

2.11 Root Cause Codes (Repair Codes)

2.11.1 Where the failure code is general in nature, the root cause code is specific. The entire code should have three numeric fields and two alpha-numeric fields to contain the information. The first three numbers will describe the operation and the (more) specific problem. The last two alpha-numeric codes will locate the failure on the specific tool. The engineering department assigns location based on an x or y axis. Use that system to locate failures. There is no need to re-invent the wheel. The following list is fairly complete (without location codes) and covers most instances of failure in a stamping operation.

See "Die PM Repair Codes" in Appendix.

2.11.2 This is not a complete listing of possible codes. It should help the workforce steering committee by providing an example of how to construct a coding system. Many facilities already own a Root Cause Analysis program and procedure. If that is the case, simply name the codes something new and understandable to the respective workforce. The codes are a very important element of the PM process and provide a simpler means to analyze present conditions while allowing comparison with previous conditions. The codes should be flexible in that they can be added to or changed to reflect unique circumstances. However, it is very easy to, rather quickly, become encumbered with a large quantity of codes that only provide minutia – as opposed to pertinent, clear documentation of tooling failure.

2.12 Checklist Development

2.12.1 The workforce steering committee (WSC) must also ensure that every tool has an appropriate checklist to govern the type of activities performed during each tool's cycle-based PM procedure. As noted earlier, a generic checklist can be assigned to each tool as it enters the production environment. The PM procedure (task list) for each tool is the most important document in the process. Simply put, the task list must reflect the tool. Only procedures that support activities performed by the tool should be on the list. As previously stated, trades people should develop a generic checklist for each type of tool. Most draw dies have common features and components. So too, the trim die and flange die. Starting with the generic list and modifying the list for each and every die as it ages in the program will benefit the desired outcome. As the tool ages within the system, the generic checklist can be customized. Adding activities to reflect actual die design or deleting activities that are not applicable. If a die begins at the 50,000 cycle schedule, the checklist should be fully customized by the fourth (200,000 cycle) scheduled PM procedure. The customization can be based on comments from those who actually perform the check. Some trim dies do punching, some pierce dies do flanging, and so on. Capture each activity and every component on this list. It is very efficient and cost effective to prevent lost time due to searching for something that does not exist or, conversely, it is very costly to not service a critical component that does not appear on the list. The maintenance staff must be made aware of their importance to the success of the process. They work with the tools and they are the only ones who know what must be done to keep the tool in tip-top shape. It is these craft people who ultimately control the content of each PM checklist.

2.12.2 The WSC should make arrangements to save the (hard-copy) PM Checklist as a controlled document (a la TS16949-20XX). A three-ring binder is enough trouble to go to. It is counter-productive to record the completed checklist in the computer. But, it is important to preserve and use the accumulated checklists for the 1,000,000 hit, or earlier, tool evaluation. Eventually, a process will be implemented to properly assign the appropriate cycle for scheduling any PM procedure.

2.12.3 In addition to the specific checks, there are common tasks that should be performed whenever a tool comes to the maintenance area. Things like washing, re-charging cylinders, scrap removal, bolt tightening: common tasks that should be completed or checked at every level, every time. The logical place for this list is right with the die-specific list. It's an easy task to attach common procedures onto the specific PM sheet and it reinforces the concept of total responsible maintenance. Check build-ups for broken screws, as an example. Clean every die and alternate which die is cleaned so that every time your workforce is cleaning a different die. Cleaning is, probably, the most important activity that takes place during any maintenance procedure. It reveals cracked components, loose welds, broken screws and components, slivers, slugs, etc. Steam booths are handy to have and make cleaning quick and easy. Another common task is to re-lubricate the guidance components just prior to the tool's return to the press. There are many common tasks and they should be listed on the backside of the PM Checklist or posted on a large sign in the maintenance area for all to see and follow. Until the common tasks become second nature to everyone in the work crew, it may be best to provide for a check-off on the back of the PM Checklist. That way, the PM Coordinators can verify that the process is working and that these important procedures are being finished.

2.12.4 Is a picture worth a thousand words? Usually it is. Whatever increases understanding of a process should be used to reduce error and possible physical failure. Whenever one of two components must be removed to access another die detail, painting the must-remove components with red or yellow paint can work pretty well. What works much better is adding a picture or drawing that shows how the pieces interact. Computer generated graphics are so easy to produce these days; almost anyone can cobble together a suitable drawing in short order. Protected with a plastic sleeve and attached to the die, the drawing becomes an important work-aid. The same can be accomplished by using a reference tag on the die shoe that directs the die maker to a computer file or binder that contains the graphic.

2.12.5 Machine tool operation is another subject that lends itself to work-aid documents. While not explicitly PM oriented, PM is a part of maintenance and machine tools are used in the repair process. Use of a drill sharpening machine, knee-grinder, die leveler, lamina drill, Port-a-Mag©, etc. are all possible subjects of a work-aid document. The crafts are learned in many places and not everyone has met and used every tool during their career. A visual assist can safely direct people in the use of most shop equipment. This, then, becomes another responsibility of the WSC since it is composed of (generally) more experienced, higher seniority craft people who are most aware of plant assets and available equipment.

2.13 Transitional Manpower

2.13.1 Depending on the condition of the tooling when the PM program is implemented, there may be a need for more craft persons. The tooling that is being held together with duct tape and banding iron must be – probably continuously – kept repaired while the PM process is given a chance to make a significant change in general tool condition. Because it will take some time to bring the tools under control, the additional employees may be around long enough to allow workforce reduction via the more painless attrition method. Every stamping facility has to make its own decision in this regard. But… if the PM process is not fully supported by a sufficient workforce, it may not reach its full potential in a timely manner. If the results limp in and lag behind expectations, the possible politics associated with such a significant change in the work environment could be enough to destroy any chance to implement PM. It is unfortunate, but politics is a reality of any business environment. The lack of management support, in whatever form, will be used by nay-sayers to destroy craft support for the PM program. Therefore, the issue of increased manpower should be discussed at the outset of the PM program and implementation should then become a smooth and orderly expansion of the entire program.

2.13.2 As the PM program builds more and more reliability into the production process, there should be an opportunity to reduce production manpower. There should be less need for utility people to fix burred panels, act like automation, remove stubborn scrap, etc. The dies become optimized as they are PM'd and run smoother with fewer and fewer quality issues. Reliability means that there is less need for back-up stock to cover for production lost to downtime failures. Eliminating back-up stock frees up valuable floor space which can then be converted to a profitable use – like sub-assembly or more production equipment. Those displaced by a smoother running production process can be employed to populate these newly established profit centers.

2.13.3 While this chapter deals with manpower, it also must mention just-in-time (JIT) considerations. As anyone who has tried JIT knows, it is impossible to force this discipline into the production system. When the large auto manufacturers try to impose JIT on their "partners", they force them to take extra-ordinary measures to look like they comply. There are those who brag that they have done it but, truth be told, they will likely possess an off-site storage facility to house their very costly back-up panels. JIT is impossible to achieve unless the tooling is under control and the production equipment is under control. A PM program for equipment is not enough; a comprehensive tooling PM program must join it as well.

2.13.4 While the initial implementation of a tooling PM program may require hiring more craft people, look to the displaced production workers to fill attritional openings. They will (likely) need to enter an apprenticeship program to ensure that they gain the required skills to become reliable, competent craft persons. But, since they have watched the PM program develop and improve the production process, they will not need to be trained to accept the principles of PM. This approach will provide more committed workers and improve labor-management relations by affecting the attitude of people who could easily feel that their livelihoods are at risk.

2.13.5 During the transition from reactive-based maintenance to preventive-based maintenance (key word here is "based" since reactive will never go away, it can only be reduced to a very minor part of a preventive-based maintenance system), there will be a need for extra workers. There are next to none available who have worked under the discipline of a comprehensive PM program for tools and dies. It is important, therefore, that they be hired with the understanding that they are transitional and subject to being moved from one area to another as the needs of the plant demand. The number of die makers used for production trouble-shooting, for example, will be cut in half or, optimally, cut out entirely. If the newly acquired floor space results in more production stamping lines, they will be spread out to cover those needs or they may be required to join the PM workforce and cover the added dies being run in the new presses. If, instead, the floor space is converted to new-die construction, they will need basic skills such as blueprint reading, layout or machine operation. Try to get the right people with a wide range of skills when they are being hired, or plan to train them as the PM program progresses.

2.14 Supervisory Employees

2.14.1   If there is a cynical bone in the body of the plant workforce, it resides in the body of supervisors. Supervisors, team leaders, foremen, general foremen, area managers, whatever they are called, form the supervision team. They have seen it all. They have seen most of it fail and they don't expect much of it to succeed. Their attitude is another reason to provide a Champion who can provide leadership and demand compliance with management's PM initiative.

2.14.2   The process will have more chance of success if the supervisory personnel are pre-trained and given a chance to accept PM based on its inherent value; on the expectation that it will make their jobs easier. "What's in it for me" works in this situation since results can be documented sufficiently to prove its value to their individual area of responsibility. Even in union situations, workers look to and expect the leadership of their supervisor. The successful supervisor, in turn, looks for support from his team and does whatever they feel is necessary to gain the confidence and support of the crew. Of course, supervisors don't do this because they are nice people. They cultivate this relationship because they know that their "stretch goals" and production quotas are more easily attained when their crew-members support them. Management, to ensure the success of the comprehensive PM program, must exploit this relationship.

2.14.3 Supervisors are best enlightened about the value of PM, and the depth of management's commitment to its implementation, through a comprehensive educational or "training" program. These days, "training" has come to mean making employees aware of management objectives and how the plant manager intends to implement certain changes. This is good. This method leaves little ambiguity about the goals and methods envisioned by the most important person in the plant.

2.15 Training Needs

2.15.1 The current employees are probably well aware of many plant practices. Many will have minor misconceptions about a practice or two, but, generally, all are on the same page of the operations manual. When the transitional workforce is hired, there will be an opportunity to provide training and re-training for the entire workforce. New members will be made aware of plant practices and individual expectations. Older employees will be made aware of what is coming in the area of changes to accommodate a comprehensive PM program. But, what do they need to know? How can management best use a training program?

2.15.2 There are a number of avenues that can be explored. First, of course, there is the knowledgeable training consultant who can spend the time necessary to interview management, supervisors and members of the workforce to arrive at a workable approach. There is also the workshop route to take. Ask the employee what they feel would be best. That involves a thorough explanation of the program, its possibilities and impossibilities, as well as the outlook for the future of the affected manufacturing facility. Never underestimate the expertise of the workforce members – especially the workforce steering committee. Their day to day involvement in the operation of the plant and the production process, gives them particular insight into the problems and the solutions that concern their work assignment.

2.15.3 A combined approach will also work: a knowledgeable consultant who uses a workshop approach to identify training needs. Whatever is decided, everyone involved must know what is expected of them; who is responsible for the management of the process; and why they are involved in yet another management project. Training is the way and its place is right at the program implementation phase.

2.15.4   As previously stated, the supervisor is an essential element that is necessary to the success of the PM initiative. They must be re-trained in order to become a change-agent. When they were hired, they were either instructed to impose a discipline on the workforce under their care or they were allowed to form their own supervisory technique. Whichever happened, it is no longer a viable method to employ. The rules have changed and they must be convinced that the new PM rules are authentic and, with their help, will form the basis of a new plant culture. A culture that will allow the company to earn more profit, accept new work, employ more workers, improve quality, increase their impact on the manufacturing process, and bring employment security and advancement opportunity to them on a personal basis.

2.15.5   Even though the workers will be trained in the new PM process and even though they may be convinced of its value, it will be up to the supervisor to reinforce the principals of PM that were taught in the classroom. The supervisor must be aware of the process of checklist development, the various codes, and the need for inputting data in a timely manner, and their responsibility to accurately record and describe every maintenance activity that takes place during their hours of employment. If the data input clerk (or coordinator) is missing from work on any particular day, the supervisor must be aware enough to appoint someone else to take over the task. If the PM sheets keep coming in way too clean, they must care enough to follow up and make sure the PMs are actually being done. In short, the supervisor must be made aware of how and why the entire workforce, and particularly their crew, should support the PM initiative.

2.15.6   One way to re-train the supervisors is to speak to their wallet. Every supervisor is controlled, to some extent, by the goals set for them with their immediate supervisor or manager. In most facilities, goals must be met – or a significant attempt must have been made to achieve those goals – before any talk of a salary increase can begin. Failure to achieve goals results in fewer and lower pay increases as well as lost opportunities for advancement. For this reason, setting a certain level of participation in the tooling PM program will greatly influence the supervisor's commitment to PM. A pre-determined increase in tooling reliability or a decrease in production downtime should be part of the goal setting activity. There should be little doubt about management's commitment to PM. There should be no doubt about management's expectations of each supervisor's involvement in making sure that a comprehensive PM program succeeds at their plant, on their watch.

2.15.7 The team concept is a proven winner in the manufacturing environment. The successful area manager/foreman knows that team formation involves more than getting a few people together to do some work. Individual interest and ability should determine what role each team member plays in the overall maintenance plan. Repairing a slugged punch/post, for example, requires someone who has skill and patience. Optimizing the use of electronic monitoring equipment needs someone with above-average technical skills. The supervisor that is placed in charge of this type of team must be aware of each person's skill level and disposition toward work.

2.15.8 Craft people with weak skills can be trained. Attitudes can be counseled. Insecurities can be re-assured. The area manager will identify these weaknesses and work to improve the team while imparting management's need to stabilize the production process while improving quality and raising production throughput. Later in this book, formation of a team that spans all the shifts in a plant will be discussed. At that point, the superintendent will come into play – or the Champion, if it is a different person. Obviously, everyone has a role to play and a responsibility to accept when a comprehensive tooling PM program is adopted and implemented.

2.16 Manpower Allocation

2.16.1 Because this and every business strategy is about saving or making money, the sooner that management sees results the better. In fact, if the strategy included using a target production line and the tooling assigned to that line, then the first savings can be obtained there. The PM program is proven effective and the tooling is being brought under control. If a trouble-shooter is assigned to that line, add a second line for them to watch since the demands against their time are much less on the original line. Of course, this strategy works best if the second line being attacked is right next to the first. Eventually, as reliability comes to the entire press room, at least half of the attending die makers can be re-assigned to either added production areas or to a completely new profit center. Later, a strategy to completely eliminate all on-line trouble-shooters will be explained. It will occur much later in the development of the tooling PM program.

2.16.2   Moving, or reallocating, manpower can be a very sensitive area. People build "homes" at their workplace and settle in. Disrupting the status quo will cause some consternation since (1) people don't want to move and (2) a change may mean that someone will lose their job. This situation is tailor-made for a supervisor to handle. The seemingly negative situation will be at the mercy of the supervisor's rapport with the crew. The outcome will rely on the supervisor's integrity and ability to properly communicate with their crew members. Their rapport, their integrity and their ability to communicate will be governed by how much information has been consistently provided to the workers and by how much the workforce has been involved in the development of the PM program.

2.16.3   In fact, the re-allocation of workers should be part of the general conversation during the developmental stages of PM. When people expect the coming changes and know that their jobs will not be in jeopardy, they will actually look forward to the opportunity to do something different or to the change of scenery. As it is throughout each phase of the PM program implementation, the supervisors are key players in a successful effort.

2.17 Preventive Maintenance Schedule

2.17.1   Another basic element on the PM process is the PM schedule. Actually there are two schedules. The first schedule to develop is the year long, week by week, "proof" that all tools can be accommodated and serviced in the PM program. The second schedule is a working document that actually shows the date when the next expected PM is to be performed – and the actual dates that show when each PM was accomplished.

2.17.2 Both types of PM schedule are to be based on cycle frequency. Based on the process and on the production requirements, a frequency cycle must be established that reflects a reasonable approach to maintaining the tools in an optimum condition. Once the cycle frequency is established, it is easy to project dates when each tool should be ready for PM. For example: if the manufacturer projects sales of 100K refrigerators a year and the dies that make the front (or any) panel are on a 25K cycle frequency, then the schedule should show dates that are three months apart. The schedule is tied to the production count.

2.17.3 Do not start counting from the date of the last PM because then the discipline of the system quickly becomes lost. Stick to the cycle frequency and execute four PMs a year for a die that produces 100K parts a year. If a PM is two weeks late and that causes the next PM to be moved two weeks back and that will happen across the entire die population, the planning schedule will become meaningless.

2.17.4 The supervisor will be tempted to delay bringing a tool into the maintenance area based on the workload, hoping to fudge a little extra time by putting off a PM activity. This "reasonable" fudging is supported by the performance of the tool. But, the changing of cycle frequency – and this surely is a change – must be subject to an analysis that is based on the performance of the tool as it regards cycle-frequency, pressroom failures and downtime. That extra time will disappear because the next tool is coming up to its time for PM. So… the only way for the errant supervisor to save time is to eliminate the PM altogether and hope that it makes it to the next scheduled PM. Generally, skewing the cycle frequency makes the collected data mostly meaningless. There are other ways to expedite the scheduling of PMs without damaging the system. These alternate methods will be discussed later in the chapters.

2.17.5 The first step to determine cycle frequency is to determine how critical the part produced is to the final assembly. Obviously, outer panels are more critical than braces and other hidden parts. A burr or a slight deformation will definitely be a problem with the surface panel. A support bracket can have a few burrs and slight surface deformation without affecting the hidden performance of the part produced. These two failures on two different parts demonstrate the criticality of cycle frequency. The outer panel may perform trouble free for 60K hits (supporting a 50K hit schedule) while the bracket will be satisfactory for 112K hits (supporting a 100K hit schedule). Or not.

2.17.6 Another consideration is the tool itself. A simple "clunker" re-strike die has few moving parts and little opportunity to fail. A five-slide forming die for a hood, however, can have two aerial slides, two lower slides and a collapsing post with a combined flanging line of 200 plus inches. Lots can go wrong in this operation. Caution dictates that this die should be looked at on a more regular basis and, even though failures do not occur on a regular basis, it is wiser to spend the time and check this one on a shorter cycle frequency schedule.

2.17.7 In a tight labor market, it may not be possible to hire sufficient craft people to support the desired PM schedule. To accommodate this lack of manpower, extending cycle frequency will be necessary. Although this situation will not provide an optimum solution to a problematic production operation, it will definitely improve the process. In the meantime, offering apprenticeships to current, non-skilled employees will improve employee morale and improve the prospects for enlarging the skilled workforce in the future.

2.17.8 To better understand the meaning of maintenance costs, as the maintenance program is being built from the ground up, there is one step that should be taken. It is not absolutely necessary but it can prove to be invaluable. Dies/tooling should be rated by complexity. Situations differ but, generally, a 1 − 5 rating system will work and it can be based on the type of die (form, flange, trim, prog); components (upper/lower cams, pads, springs, etc); and what part was produced by the die as well (the surface for a fender die needs more care than one for a cross-member). It will provide the ability to track maintenance time/cost by die complexity and determine how much time is spent maintaining the die as opposed to disassembly and assembly procedures. It is not unusual for a die to take two full shifts x three die makers just to disassemble. Sometimes for a simple fix, sometimes not, but the potential is that it will take as much time to repair as it does to take the die apart. Someone, somewhere thinks they are saving a load of money by combining several operations into a single die. With a collection of this type of data, feedback can be provided to the die designer – another TS16949-20XX requirement.

2.17.9 There are other opportunities. One that the comptroller will appreciate: the ability to accurately budget maintenance costs at the point when a die enters the production plant. Also, maintenance hours for each tool can be compared to the model; attention can be drawn to such issues as bad design, lack of proper maintenance equipment, poor scheduling practices, etc.; manpower allocations can be adjusted; and the real value of a comprehensive PM program can be determined by its affect on the entire plant operation.

2.17.10 Whether the checklist is generic, in the case of a new die, or customized, for a longer running tool, it must be available before it can be effectively used. When computers are readily available on the shop floor, it is a simple matter for the die maker to quickly check the die's status for cycle-based PM and print out an existing check sheet. Barring that possibility, the effective method must rely on physical, hard-copy checklists. These can be prepared at the beginning of each month or week and kept in a binder and available to every one on every shift. A procedure can be established that provides for routine referral to the checklist binder to see if a die that's in the maintenance area for repair might also need to be PM'd. This procedure may seem to treat PM as a casual practice. It merely recognizes that there is an economy that can and should be achieved in every aspect of the maintenance program.

2.17.11 Preparing die PM checklists in advance also allows the supervisory personnel to schedule their work in a more efficient manner. Requests for release time to perform more difficult PM checks are their responsibility. Assigning sufficient personnel to ensure completion before die set is another. The supervisor's role in distributing PM checklists is so important to the success of a PM program that participation should be rated and included in their annual salary review.

2.17.12 There are two fields of thought on recording checklists. One is to enter each completed procedure into the computer maintenance management system and evaluate the effectiveness of the program by counting the number of checklist items that were accomplished. Another approach is to keep the checklist process on paper – entering the date of completion on the aforementioned PM schedule. This approach requires that every item on the check sheet must be finished before the supervisor or die maker turns in the checklist.

2.17.13 Every PM checklist must be reviewed at one time or another. Therefore, it must be retained. To comply with TS16949-20XX standards, they can be time/date stamped before filing away. "Away" does not mean transfer to some remote location for a specified time period before disposal. Checklists are best stored in a binder, together by specific die/tool. They are the principle means of die evaluation at pre- determined steps. The step, dependant on actual throughput, might be scheduled on a more or less annual basis. Higher production dies will dictate a semi-annual review. This review will be cycle-based and it will concern itself with die performance and reliability. If the die, for example, prospers under a 50,000 cycle PM schedule, with only one or two unscheduled repair occurrences, then it should be considered a candidate for placement on a 75,000 or 100,000 cycle schedule. The tactic is to PM as often as necessary, but no more than necessary.

2.17.14 If things are done right, everything will change. Consistent performance re-evaluation will be normal and necessary. Increasing cycle times (from 50k to 100k for example) will mean lower maintenance cost. But, if the incidents of repair or downtime increase, it will be time to backtrack to a previous cycle. Incidents of repair, the type of repair and any incident of downtime accumulation will be part of the evaluation process. Set guidelines and stick to them. Written rules and procedures, strictly followed, will provide the opportunity to fine-tune the PM process.

2.17.15 The review process, coupled with a realistic scheduling program, will eventually indicate that more production can be handled by the press room. Careful shopping for additional parts – using die complexity to forecast probable PM and repair time requirements – can be used to add the profitable "fill" to the plant's production schedule.

2.18 PM Training

2.18.1 Everyone in the plant is a candidate for training in the requirements for the successful, implementation of a tooling PM process. Obviously, the most highly trained individual is the PM Coordinator, followed by the Champion. Nuts and bolts information should be shared with every trade person and their supervisor. The production worker, production supervisor, and every manager must have a working knowledge of what PM is and how it will affect their role in the plant infrastructure.

2.18.2 There is very little training available for a tooling PM coordinator. Mostly because there is very little tooling PM being done. The conventional wisdom dictates that PM is a waste of time and resources when applied to a unique tool that has a limited life-span. For this reason, the tooling PM coordinator must pursue training in the general principles of equipment PM and adapt the knowledge to apply it to tools and dies. Understanding equipment PM will provide a leg-up in the process of understanding tooling PM. The exact same principles apply. Periodic checks, checklists, reviews, common tasks, documented practices, are all fundamental to the PM process.

2.18.3 Several universities are involved in the preventive/predictive maintenance industry. The military and the energy companies are primary supporters of PM technology and can direct the interested individual to the nearest source of PM training. It is important to remember that the knowledge acquired at these various sessions is subject to interpretation and re-application according to the conditions present in the individual production facility.

2.18.4 The PM Coordinator must also be trained in the use of computers and the capabilities of computer software. While they will not be expected to design PM-specific software, they must be ready to provide direction in the customization of off-the-shelf software or in the design of custom designed mainframe software as the case may be. Since management support is vital to the success of the PM program, the PM Coordinator should also be trained to use charting and presentation-type software programs. Pertinent, well-composed visuals can impart relevant data as well as build confidence in the developing PM process, the role of the PM Coordinator should not be underestimated, and, the coordinator's most important role is to communicate and provide information relevant to the impact of the new maintenance initiative.

2.18.5 Hopefully, the tool & die maker will not need to be further trained in die repair techniques. Training in PM though, is another matter. Inasmuch as training is expected to inform as well as instruct, the training of skilled personnel should seek to inform them of their new responsibilities, PM's affect on their daily routine, the value that PM will add to plant operations, and, finally, what PM can do for their personal job security.

2.18.6 For the PM initiative to be successful, the skilled trades person must provide input – based on their expertise – to be recorded regarding the condition of the tooling as well as their assessment of the actual reason for failures experienced during the production operation. While their skills are needed to provide the appropriate repair, their input is also vital to the on-going success of the program. Their understanding of the failure codes and the root cause codes will form the basis by which meaningful reviews can take place that will improve the tooling, the production process and, ultimately, the design process that results in hard tooling for production.

2.18.7 A clear understanding of how PM can change their daily responsibilities without threatening their employment status is necessary to retain their good will and elicit the enthusiastic support necessary to the implementation of the PM process. A die maker will appreciate the fact that management is trying to eliminate the occurrence of failures that require their climbing into the stamping press to affect some minor or major repair. Climbing into a stamping press is a dangerous situation and one that should be avoided if at all possible. The fact that PM's objective is to eliminate this dangerous situation will not be lost on the average die maker. This bit of information should be a basic message during the training schedule of all skilled trade persons.

2.18.8 When tooling is reliable and produces quality parts, management's imagination goes into overdrive. Increasing floor space provides opportunities, for sure, but the need to stop the presses and wait for a repair to be not too quickly accomplished may have to be re-considered in light of another opportunity: quick die change (QDC). Once reserved only for the small, single part die, QDC can be a possibility for large multi-die operations. Properly designed, very few minutes are lost during a complete changeover and start-up for a different part. With the die out of the press, an effective, properly prepared repair can be accomplished – further protecting the integrity of the die components. The key here is that QDC depends on reliability. Reliability depends on a comprehensive PM program.

2.18.9 The natural by-product of PM is reliability. The ability to produce quality parts in sufficient quantity to satisfy production requirements without use of an over-supply of buffer parts. No buffer parts mean that space is available to add other profit centers – more jobs. Reliability also means more capacity on the existing lines of presses. To the trade person, reliability should mean job security. Relaying this pertinent information regarding job security is a proper subject for a trainer to deliver.

2.18.10 Once considered an expendable commodity, today's manufacturing environment has turned the production worker into a valuable asset. Training used to take five or ten minutes at the start of their first day of employment. Now it takes that long to explain how to enter the plant using a key card. New technology has forced manufacturers to spend training dollars in order to maximize the use of new equipment and methods that allow competition in the international marketplace.

2.18.11 PM training should be a part of the training for production workers. They should be trained as observers, catching quality flaws as early as possible, identifying malfunctioning equipment, and, then, stopping the presses to prevent any further failures and malfunctions from occurring. They, also, should be aware of their changing environment. Reliability may mean that the production crew will not move to another line to keep busy. It may also mean that production runs will decrease and they will be expected to help with changeovers, for example. The workforce should also be informed that increased reliability would mean more work and more jobs.

2.18.12 The production supervisor should be made aware of the structure and goals of the PM program. Training is the obvious vehicle to accomplish this awareness. Compared to everyone else, the PM program will make the most difference in his or her work life. During the initial phase of the PM initiative, they should expect improvements and increased throughput and react to them by increasing their expectations and the expectations of their crew. Being trained in what to expect from the new process will enable them to provide the vital feedback that is required to move the PM program toward successful implementation and to enable them to properly instruct their crewmembers concerning their particular areas of responsibility.

2.18.13 It is the production supervisors' responsibility to record occurrences of failure during the production run – and to record them accurately. As previously stated, only by using the codes when recording failures will the system be accurate. The supervisor can give that goal a giant leap forward by insisting on accuracy from whomever they assign to the task.

2.18.14 Another thing that they should do is quickly review the tooling when it returns to the press after a PM checklist activity. This serves as a check and balance on slipshod or careless work – or no work - being done during the scheduled PM. The review process should be concerned with an improvement to the panel being produced. Better trim edges, cleaner flanges, etc. should be the normal result of a proper PM. The review will also make them aware of incidental damage being done to the tooling during the movement and die-set process. The form can be easily produced in MS Word© and could look like this:

See "Feedback Form Example" in Appendix.

2.18.15 The discipline of using this type of form, while necessary during the implementation phase, should be determined by the key players on the shop floor: the production supervisor and the trade, or skilled, supervisor. Use of the form may raise an issue that should be addressed. The types of issue that should be reported, where to return the form to ensure proper disposition, and exactly what constitutes a remedy are all topics for discussion at a joint meeting of production and skilled supervisors.

2.18.16 Acting as leader of the skilled workforce, the skilled supervisor should receive training similar to the PM Coordinator. They need a basic understanding of the principles of PM, predictive maintenance (PdM) and total productive maintenance (TPM). It is not enough that they know the benefits of these initiatives. They must become advocates and constantly search for opportunities to expand the program and improve each step of the process. Their salary reviews must contain elements of PM to gauge their participation and leadership. Since TPM is the ultimate goal, they must seek opportunities to move PM to PdM. As stated earlier, PdM relies on some form of electronic measurement to indicate a degree of wear that forecasts failure. The enthusiastic skilled supervisor will search for possible venues to share electronic devices, used by the equipment PdM industry, to start a rudimentary PdM program.

2.18.17 Make no mistake. PdM is not a vital part of PM. It is just the opposite. PM is a vital component of PdM. However, remaining aware of where the tooling maintenance program must proceed will actually better determine the necessary PM activities and help evaluate their impact on the overall maintenance process. The skilled supervisor brings valuable experience to the entire maintenance process. Training will help direct their enthusiasm as well as use their experience to the best advantage.

2.18.18 As the PM program matures; there is a final step that could be taken. Work teams can be assigned to maintain specific dies. If the operation is such that multiple shifts and crews are present, strive to assign specific tooling to specific teams. One approach would be to start with a team for a specific set of production lines and then continue to define smaller work teams until teams of two from each shift are assigned to work on specific sets of tooling. Their responsibilities would encompass PM, reactive maintenance and quality improvement. In short, if the tooling fails during the production run – they would fix it; if the panel is burred – they sharpen trim steels between die sets; if a PM cycle occurs – they perform the checklist. This team should know the tooling assigned to them better that anyone else.

2.18.19 An added advantage associated with this step is a self-directed workforce. Proper communication between trade people and between shifts eliminates the need for further direction. Supervisory personnel should be used for more productive work like expediting workflow between work crews and departments such as machinists and welders. Let them plan and follow-up on engineering changes and quality fixes from the customer. Supervisors must oversee the entire process: make sure that repairs are completed; data is entered into an appropriate database; and that periodic review takes place where each piece of tooling is properly analyzed. A good training program, at the beginning of the PM initiative, will be of great advantage to the supervisor who can then grow with the PM program as it slowly becomes the existing paradigm within their manufacturing facility.

2.18.20 If there is anyone who does not need extensive training in PM, it must be the manager. Every step being made in a comprehensive tooling PM program does not have to be revealed to the management team. They should be aware that the PM program is progressing and that certain results are being achieved. They do not have to know that six dies were PM'd today. Their training, however, should apprise them of what to expect, and when, regarding program development and deployment. Managers will make up the PM program review team. For that reason, metrics, report formats and charting choices must be determined and approved by these managers. It is their training and their consultants that will lead them to choose the proper evaluation tools.

2.18.21 As previously stated, "the most highly trained individual is the PM Coordinator, followed by the Champion." During the initial educational (not training) phase, the Champion and the PM Coordinator should be "Burns and Allen", "Mutt and Jeff", "Tom & Jerry". In a word: inseparable. It is crucial that both of them possess a complete understanding of the costs and rewards, methods and expectations inherent to a successful PM process.

2.18.22 This partnership must become a cooperative alliance that seeks common goals through the consistent application of PM tools. The Coordinator must gather pertinent data and ensure its accuracy. The Champion must determine the relevant metric and present the charts that will garner support from the members of management staff. The Coordinator will survey needs and determine what tools will be required to support PM. The Champion will lobby the Plant Manager and Comptroller to expedite the purchase of this essential equipment. The Coordinator may identify appropriate educational opportunities, but the Champion must obtain the financial support to fund their education. Again, they are a team.

2.18.23 Most seminars that deal with PM contain practical, working knowledge and a management perspective as well. Getting the "other side" (labor/supervisory/managerial) will help each of them to better understand possibilities and expectations while they personally form the context of their plant's individual PM program requirements. Tompkins Associates and Saddle Island Institute are sources of training for PM.

2.19 Role Definition/Work Assignments

2.19.1 Before there is an effort to establish any type of sea-change in a plant's operation, it is a good idea to establish a responsibility chart. Who is responsible for the (insert type) activity? Compiling the document can be seen as developing a "fault" list. Management, specifically the owner/plant manager, will decide if that is the way to proceed. Usually, that method simply perpetuates the old system. "That's the way we've done it for years" is the usual statement that fronts for an abusive and repressive management. This approach to maintenance will change every person's role in the production process. In a word, that makes PM rather scary. Concerns for job security, bruised ego (someone actually believed in the "old way"), and a changing role will unsettle many in the workplace. It is best to allay some fears and, at least, pre-determine each person's role in the new method of achieving productive stability.

2.19.2 The Workforce Steering Committee and a manager should meet to discuss and determine the role of every type of individual that is concerned with tooling and equipment maintenance in the manufacturing facility. What is the role and authority of the PM Coordinator(s)? Does the Champion have a final decision-making ability that transcends the Plant Manager? Limited how? The skilled workers will have more responsibility than the production workers and their supervisors. Is the skilled supervisor best used as a cop or as a program planner and scheduler? How should the plant manager/owner interact with the various functionaries and the workforce to optimize results from a comprehensive PM program?

2.19.3 The answers to the foregoing questions must be determined and properly recorded - if not posted. Common sense and the facility's normal operating procedures are the main factors to be used when engaging in this exercise. Adherence to the enunciated responsibilities must be enforced by management practice, including a prominent consideration during salary review sessions at the supervisory and management levels.

2.19.4 The primary responsibility for the successful implementation of a PM program resides with the PM Coordinator. The coordinator must exercise leadership and authority commensurate with that of a manager. That may seem like a lot of authority to confer onto what may be an hourly-paid person. However, waiting for someone else to "direct" another department to provide basic needs to the PM office and staff will cause the program to flounder and stall. Likewise, if every detail of every proposal must be cleared before implementation can be accomplished. That is not to say that the PM Coordinator can act unilaterally. Constant communication is absolutely required between the coordinator and the Champion. But, the Champion should only interfere when basic program goals are in danger.

2.19.5 Immersion in the program will result in a clearer understanding of PM program development than any other person in the plant. The coordinator will recognize weaknesses and excesses, growth opportunities and plan failures. It is a natural occurrence that the new PM program will receive intense scrutiny from all corners of the company – and well it should. It is imperative, though, that failure and other problems (deployment, materials, etc.) be successfully dealt with within a short time frame. Everyone will understand that adjustments must be made in a new program, but, allowing problems to go unanswered is like experiencing a lingering, ghastly death. Almost everyone, suddenly, wants to go and be elsewhere.

2.19.6 The office staff should be led by the Coordinator, adjusting data input and altering data collection as the program develops. PM staff will produce the checklists and distribute them to the appropriate supervisor. They will edit checklist content according to the suggestions and direction of the skilled workforce. They must also be properly trained in the principles of PM and familiar with repair shop practices since they will provide the primary data-input activity unless/until that task is eventually shifted to the skilled workforce. All of this should be under the purview of the PM Coordinator.

2.19.7 In addition, the Coordinator will be responsible for ensuring that:

- All basic data for each tool in the production area is collected and entered into the database;
- The list of tools, identified by the steering committee, that are needed by the skilled workers are procured and provided to the maintenance areas;
- Checklists and evaluations are available for audit by management;
- Progress and other periodic reports are compiled for the edification of all concerned;
- New technologies and improved procedures are studied and deployed as they are discovered.
- Acting as the liaison, the concerns of management and the workforce are quickly and effectively answered and that the solutions, if any, are acquired and deployed.

2.19.8 These passages are by no means the entire list of possible responsibilities that can be assigned to the Coordinator. They are, however, important to consider and the basis for identifying a likely suspect to fill the role of PM Coordinator.

2.20 Skilled Trade Person

2.20.1 Simply put, the trade person must perform the actual work. Obviously, they are also the source to consult when identifying what work should be done. They use the checklist during a tool PM. The skilled worker will identify unnecessary procedures and ask that others be added to address the needs of components that are not included in a "generic" checklist.

2.20.2 The entire "Root Cause Code" and "Failure Code" lists will be developed for their use. The die maker's ability, inspection and experience will determine the code that they assign to any failure experienced during production as well as during the subsequent inspection at the maintenance area. In large part, the success of the PM program rests on their attention to detail and their willingness to properly document their PM activities.

2.21 Skilled Trade Supervisor

2.21.1 It is up to the skilled trade supervisor to ensure that maintenance and repairs are accomplished in an economical manner; that they are returned to specification and/or repaired using quality materials and effective work procedures; and that each skilled worker has the necessary materials and training to accomplish their daily tasks. Their close personal knowledge of each tool under their control can be used to further expedite the process.

2.21.2 As the primary reviewer of tooling, they can be expected to initiate quality improvements as well as suggest extending or shortening the cycle based PM schedule for individual tools. As the person who is most aware of the capabilities of the trade persons under their direction, the supervisor will decide who does what by simple job assignment.

2.21.3 Of course, assigning a job to a capable trade person is only the beginning. If the best way to maintain each and every die is by performing routine PM procedures on each and every die, then, it seems logical to insist that every repair be accomplished in a similar manner. Preparation for welding a steel section or a composite should be uniform (pre-heat, post-heat, proper rod selection, etc.). Mil finishes for forming steels is another area that can be standardized. Across the board use of circle-grid analysis techniques and measures to determine an acceptable draw operation is another. PM is maintenance. The primary purpose of PM is to improve maintenance and the PM initiative can and should be used by an enthusiastic supervisor to drive improvements throughout the entire maintenance process.

2.22 Production Worker

2.22.1 The production worker's part to play in the PM process is one of careful handling and close inspection. Identifying failures in a timely manner can prevent an excess of scrap. Re-working panels is expensive and time-consuming. Stopping the transfer press before too many bad panels are produced is extremely important. Controlling this loss in a tandem press line is equally important. Alertness on the part of a production hand can pinpoint the failure, the offending die or component as well as reduce the loss from a less than perfect process.

2.23 Production Supervisor

2.23.1 Optimizing the production process with controlled quality and maximized throughput is the primary responsibility of the production supervisor. That's what PM is all about. This supervisor just needs to attend to business such as: reporting failures, suggesting process improvements, and inspecting repairs when dies are returned to line. All of these tasks will serve to improve and sustain the PM process.

2.24 Manager Level

2.24.1 Managers can drive the implementation of PM by insisting that PM measures be included in salary reviews for all supervisors under their direction. Armed with a basic understanding of PM and the plant manager/owner's goals concerning PM implementation, a good, common-sense list of metrics can be established that will determine the level of support displayed by the individual supervisor on an annual basis.

2.24.2 Joining with the Champion, each manager can seek to facilitate PM by: approving appropriate purchases of essential material; providing an adequate workforce to perform the PM procedures; supporting the acquisition of new tools and electronic equipment to enable workers to perform their jobs more easily and more effectively. The manager must also develop an understanding of the data reflected by the charts and graphs that have been prepared by the PM Coordinator.

2.24.3 The manager should seek a periodic meeting with the PM Coordinator. This meeting should be used to enlighten both of them regarding the other's plans and interest in the developing maintenance program. Elements of mutual benefit should be discussed. These opportunities for support and interaction must be manifest and action plans should be developed. The PM Coordinator needs the reasoned support of every member of the management team just as much as they need the cooperation of the Line and General Supervisor.

2.25 The Champion

2.25.1 The Champion is the primary player for PM on the management staff. They keep the Controller aware of the program's progress so that money is always available for reasonable purchase of material and manpower to support PM. They interact with the production manager to ensure that PM is having a positive affect on production throughput without undue downtime and that there always remains an emphasis on accurate recording of time associated with failure (codes). They interact with the facilities manager to ensure that necessary equipment is in repair and available for use by the maintenance crew, that adequate space is allocated to PM activity based on an expanding program. They interact with design management to ensure that the department will avoid designing failure into a tool using the newly available data. They interact with the plant manager to ensure that plant policy is included in the PM program and that the reports from the PM Coordinator are relevant to the needs of the plant manager's staff.

2.25.2 Inasmuch as the PM program is developing; the Champion can provide little in the way of PM counsel to the Coordinator. They both are learning as they go, so to speak. But, the Champion can act as a political mentor to the Coordinator. The habits, interests and idiosyncrasies of many managers can be a minefield for the inexperienced PM Coordinator. It is up to the Champion to provide leadership and run interference in the front office.

2.25.3 Given that the first priority of the Champion and the Coordinator is to provide an efficient and effective maintenance program to support the production operation. The second priority of the Coordinator is to support the Champion with reports that include reliable, relevant data displayed in appropriate charts. The second priority of the Champion is to support the Coordinator by pleading the case for PM at the management level and acquiring all that is needed from managers of each department to support the PM initiative.

2.26 Plant Manager/Owner

2.26.1 Visible and certain support for the PM program is the first order of business for the plant manager/owner (PMO). This program represents a complete change in the way business is conducted on the plant floor. It will be pursued only if the PMO believes its implementation will benefit the profit-making potential of the facility. Once that premise is accepted as fact, there is no reason to waver or restrain a concerted effort to implement the PM program. At staff meetings, the needs of the PM program must be considered on a par with any other plant initiative. The carefully selected Champion deserves moral and financial support. Other members of staff must be encouraged to participate and provide meaningful support to the entire maintenance program.

2.26.2 The primary benefit that the PMO can provide is a close scrutiny. Promising more than can be delivered is a common trait in today's manufacturing environment. PM can deliver outstanding results. As with any "pet project", it can also be prostituted to support the career aspirations of the up-and-coming junior executive or, conversely, to cover the shortcomings of the aging manager while they bide their time before retirement. The PMO must demand accurate data, appropriate charts and graphs, and complete reports on a regular, scheduled basis.

2.26.3 Actually, the PM program will flourish under close, but fair, scrutiny. It will meet reasonable expectations in the short term and outpace every expectation in the long term – if everyone does their job.

2.27 Workspace Allocation

2.27.1 Before proceeding with the deployment of a comprehensive tooling PM program, some consideration can be paid to the work environment as it pertains to efficiency. This habitat for two (on each shift) should meet almost all the needs of a specialized workforce: size and layout to safely accommodate the resident dies; tool/die storage in close proximity to the work cell; availability of precision measuring instruments; existing manpower; and easily understood job assignment.

2.27.2 In many cases, today's repair area looks a lot like random acts of violence. Aside from the destructive impact such a workspace has on the morale of the individual trade person, there are significant issues dealing with safety and costing that must be considered. Designing an efficient work cell and assigning specific trade people to each cell allows for better control of the repair function while it, inherently, imposes responsibility for house-keeping functions onto the assigned workers. The drawing (below) is a rough sketch of a possible work cell without the trimmings.

See "PM Workcell Layout" in Appendix.

2.27.3 Of course, safety is of paramount importance. And… safety is silently promoted by turning the workspace into "home" for the crew. When the trade person knows that they will always work in close proximity to their tool box and workbench, they tend to keep the area clean and free of unnecessary debris. Storage can be provided for spare parts, small hand tools, and various items of supply needed to maintain surface and edge on resident tooling. With everything properly stored, there is nothing underfoot to provide trip hazard or bump injury. "Clean up after yourself" is an easy policy to impose and such a policy ensures a clean, orderly and safe work area.

2.27.4 A clean, orderly and safe work area will also promote real-dollar savings. An assigned work cell can help eliminate lost details that delay pre-production assembly. The close proximity of toolboxes and storage prevents time-consuming trips in search of hand tools and precision instruments. Of course, properly outfitting each cell is a pre-requisite to the efficient operation of any repair function.

2.27.5 Ample storage cabinets for spare parts and supplies will eliminate the back and forth visits to the tool crib for frequently used items. A vending machine can be an alternative to redundant supplies of common items (i.e.: ¼" punches; grinding wheels; etc.). Close does not mean exclusive.

2.27.6 Large set-up plates can be shared by two or more work cells. Drill presses, hydraulic die separators, and hydraulic drilling machines are other examples of tools that can be shared. Layout machines can be crucial in some applications. The key is to keep such elements close to the work cell and avoid long "hunting expeditions" when such tools are needed to complete a repair or modification to a tool. Even when there is no doubt about the location of such elements, there can be several moves of the die before a crane can pick it up and deliver it to an appropriate location. Proper, careful planning of the design and location of work cells and ancillary equipment will be richly rewarded with increased efficiency.

2.27.7 Each workspace should be populated by at least two trade persons. Large or difficult tooling may require two people to separate the die shoes and dismantle the halves. Usually, it's safer and faster to work as a team. The team is not to be considered just those on the same shift. The "team" consists of all trade persons assigned to the same cell across all the shifts. This type of cell development allows the entire team to, not only, become acquainted with the tools that are normally assigned to a particular cell, but also with their counterparts on other shifts.

2.27.8 Having established a work cell that is populated with a specific work team that covers all shifts, the next logical step is to assign specific tools to be maintained by that team in that cell. Is there any better maintenance situation? A work crew that cooperates and communicates with each other, one that is familiar with the tooling through day-to-day exposure and with little need for direction from a supervisor. This is as close to a self-directed workforce as possible. This situation is only possible when tooling is properly and consistently maintained under a comprehensive tooling PM program.

2.28 Equipment Needs

2.28.1   The decision to begin a tooling PM program must be supported with a management commitment to provide the proper equipment in sufficient quantity to allow the workforce to perform their maintenance tasks without needless waiting. Properly maintained tooling may require a different sort of maintenance than is used for emergency repair operations. PM needs finesse and finish, such as small adjustments as polishing a radius with jeweler's rouge or sharpening a trim edge with a fine oilstone. Sometimes, cleaning the tool is the major contribution to quality that is achieved during a PM cycle. At other times, a complete disassemble and nitro-leak check has to be performed during the checklist activities. As the tooling improves, it may become apparent that a die set should be taken apart using hydraulic separators rather than by using the jerk and pry method. (Minor damage to trim steels caused by jerk and pry was never as apparent as they become when the tool is well maintained.)

2.28.2   All types of equipment will be impacted by PM. Some allowance should be made to provide the necessary hand tools, cranes and machine tools that will support a comprehensive PM program. It is the responsibility of the PM Coordinator and the supervisors to identify the various needs of the PM activity. It is the responsibility of management to respond to the requests for appropriate equipment.

2.28.3   When tooling improves, polishers replace hand grinders. Changes are more incremental and accurate measurement becomes more critical. Set-up plates may need to be large enough to allow room for the die as well as for the gauges that can completely check squareness and level. While the tooling becomes easier to work on, it will also respond to very small changes in position and pressure. Properly calibrated measuring devices will become ever more important to the continued success of the developing PM program.

2.28.4   Crane availability always seems to be lacking in a stamping shop. PM will require more and faster transport from storage or the production line. Complete disassembly and assembly of the die will tie-up the crane for longer periods of time. Polished form surfaces will be marred and, sometimes ruined, when turned over with uncovered chains. Adding turnover capabilities (a second crane carriage) to existing cranes will help to solve some of the problem; covering chains with protective sleeves will do the rest. Smaller gantry-type cranes can be easily added in some situations. Of course, each situation is different. But, there is a need to expect and plan for changes to the current process. Money earned due to the increased uptime provided by the PM program can be used to improve the entire maintenance operation. Cranes are an important element of the process.

2.28.5   The term capital equipment includes cranes. It also includes drill presses and saws and Difracto© equipment. It covers CNC machines and multi-axis machining capabilities. Stamping presses are also considered capital equipment. Purchase of this type of machine, requiring large amounts of capital, may seem premature. It is mentioned here, at the outset, because there must be awareness that modern, state-of-the-art equipment is not a consideration when a process is completely out of control. As the stamping process comes under control, as it surely will, the possibility to use modern transfer and tandem presses becomes more of a reality. Use of this faster, more efficient technology is a benefit of a comprehensive PM program. Optimum benefit to the stamping operation can be achieved if such an investment is made as soon as PM makes it possible.

2.29 Documents

2.29.1   Compliance with TS16949-20XX has necessitated the utilization of document control systems. Rather than starting a system early on in the development of a PM program, it may be best to wait and see how documents are created due to natural force of use. It will take a year or two of creating specialized documents to understand how and along what path the PM program will develop. Trying to number or letter or otherwise name documents prematurely will prove to be an exercise in futility.

2.29.2 Support TS16949-20XX requirements with a simple and descriptive system. "Checklist 1"; "Procedure 2"; etc. are easy and can be added onto with sequential numbering for example. That is not to say that this system is adequate over the longer term. It must eventually be re-done. Hopefully, when that time comes, the PM Coordinators will have a better idea of the needs of the PM initiative and will design an easy to remember and effective coding system.

3. Implementation

3.0.1   The groundwork has been laid. The Champion and the PM Coordinator are in place. Basic metrics have been established. The approach has been studied and the methods for implementation have been determined. The next obvious step is the implementation of a comprehensive PM program.

3.0.2   Preparation includes identifying members of the Steering Committee, adding the necessary equipment and machine tools, capturing the designated floor space, identifying code structures and assigning personnel to the tooling maintenance areas. With the foregoing items in place, the approach is finalized, staff is trained and work cells are constructed. Additional space will be needed for close-proximity storage of the tools. After that is identified, tooling can be upgraded and capital equipment may be purchased and installed.

3.1   Steering Committee

3.1.1   Whether by survey or personal experience/knowledge, potential members of the Steering Committee can be identified. These potential members are culled from: the skilled workforce; the supervisory staff of both production and skilled departments; and designees from the controller's office. The Steering Committee should make room for representatives of the equipment maintenance workforce and their supervisory staff as well as representatives from the Quality Department and Information Services. These areas should select their own representation based on whatever criteria they decide – with the understanding that they will cooperate and interact with the Steering Committee members.

3.1.2   The make-up of this committee is very important. Having members from various areas of the plant is an exploitable asset that will serve to expedite further implementation of PM. Adopting PM for tooling will profoundly affect every person and department in the facility. Each person's role in the manufacturing process is more easily defined if they, or their representative, are included in the various stages of program

3.1.3   For this reason, the Champion and the PM Coordinator should first determine who they want on the committee and, secondly, pursue those members with much energy. Begging doesn't bring positive results, but honesty, integrity and ingenuity should convince enough of the "short list" people to join the team and make a real difference in the way business is conducted at their company.

3.1.4   Every supervisor that has responsibilities within the PM impact area should want to have some participation in the Steering Committee start-up activity. Obviously, not every supervisor can spend the time required of a steering committee member. Therefore, one or two of their number should be selected to become involved with the larger committee. Those selected should have skilled trade responsibilities and involvement in the production stamping area to be most effective. While a basic knowledge of PM is helpful, it is sufficient that they accept the premise that PM is effective and will positively impact their area of responsibility. Training and inter-departmental interaction will fill in the cracks regarding their knowledge of the classic preventive maintenance regimen.

3.1.5   The greatest challenge facing the Champion and PM Coordinator is the search for committee members among the trades. Quality and work assignment is definitely a management prerogative. However, support by trade people of any initiative is crucial to success. If PM becomes just another management scheme to get the work done today, it will fail miserably. PM must become a new way of life in the plant. It will demand improved work methods, better materials, less supervision and more accountability. By selecting carefully, the right trade persons can lead by example. They are most likely to provide such leadership if they have a major part in determining the course of the PM program. That does not mean that they help set the ultimate goal of the plant. It just means that they help determine the proper road to follow to achieve success. It means that their expertise is valuable enough to be used to determine coding systems and repair procedures. That their opinions regarding tool quality and performance are sought after and honored.

3.1.6   At some point, depending on the size of the manufacturing facility, a decision will be made to add another one or two PM coordinators. After sufficient data has been collected, the analysis will dictate that certain steps should be taken to relieve troublesome aspects of dies and also to redirect design efforts to remove some perceived failure from ensuing designs of similar tools. Or, hopefully, increased efficiency can result in the addition of even more contracted part production along with the additional dies needed to produce those parts. That point is somewhat pre-determined by the Steering Committee. Not necessarily a specific date but, at least, a specific point of development in the program. This may not be an exceedingly accurate measure of need but it will serve to remind all concerned that there is a need in the future and that there should be some preparation for it in the present. Even the simple process of seeking the likely suspect will help when the time comes to appoint the next PM coordinator. This exercise also serves to establish the responsibility of the Steering Committee for a general oversight of the PM program.

3.2   Equipment Needs

3.2.1   It might be surmised that a working die maintenance area already possesses the basic tools and equipment to perform PM. Regardless; it is helpful to survey the hourly employees and ask for suggestions for additional equipment that will support a comprehensive PM program. New technology may be explored as well as the use of "makeshift" such as old bolster plates for set-up. Any appropriated area that will house the PM crew should be planned and laid-out on paper to ensure that all components are present.

3.2.2   Turn-over cranes are a necessity and there should be a sufficient number of them available. The PM Program will require additional handling of the tooling in that each die is separated and cleaned/ refurbished on a regular basis. It is foolish to begin a program – with intent to "prove" itself – and not provide adequate crane support.

The same goes for adequate die washing facilities and parts storage equipment. Will vending machines provide a resource? There are plenty of reasons and plenty of alternatives to consider. Compile a list of everything that the Steering Committee thinks is needed, determine its validity and purchase the initial equipment.

3.2.3   That is not to say that a single purchase of such tools is enough. It just means that there is recognition, by management, that a trade person needs tools and equipment to properly do their job. Identifying the proper equipment will mean that the workforce is made aware of the likely changes in their daily routine. For example: sharpening and polishing will become more normal than weld and fit or replacement activities. A survey of the skilled workforce will identify the various needs for tools and supplies and determine what quantities of each. Some are easily shared. Some others might require an individual supply.

3.2.4   Using technology to maintain tooling might seem like a waste of time when implementing a PM program while the process is completely out of control. However, consider the future. A future where mayhem is not the rule. Surface coatings, imaging hardware and software are but two examples of (somewhat) new technology. Industry-specific magazines are resources that are used to identify new ideas and processes. Manufacturer's reps are willing allies who can educate the members of the Steering Committee as well as the general workforce.

3.2.5   Lots of tools have been designed, over the years, to make life and work easier for skilled trade people. Magnet-based drilling machines and die-separators are but two examples of such devices. The task is to make sure that these tools are available in sufficient numbers to avoid long waits by valuable employees. Only one portable diffracto machine is used by only one die maker. A large population of body dies would demand that more such machines are available to facilitate surface repairs. Even mundane tools such as ratchet wrenches should be available to expedite screw removal. Or torque wrenches. Etc.

3.2.6   Makeshift is just that. Make tooling aids from available materials – usually scrap – and employ them in a productive fashion. Old bolster plates of sufficient size are recycled into use as set-up plates. Entire die sets can be set on such plates and leveled prior to reworking trim or flange steels or re-setting of punches and button sets. Smaller plates are used on benches for smaller work or to square up or check sections prior to installation into the die. Ordinarily, every repair shop is rife with such tools. The problem is that these "tools" are usually small. There is no law against making and using big tools as well. Posting a "If we only had a…" list on the company bulletin board will bring ample suggestions for such tooling aids.

3.2.7   It is necessary to restrict the use and locations of certain equipment. Precision layout equipment is just such a tool. It does have a limited use – making it a candidate for a work center as opposed to general distribution. It does need special care – proper operation of precision equipment responds in a positive manner relative to accuracy and reliability. With this in mind, then, it seems proper to establish (a) work center(s) – small shops need one and larger shops may need several. A work center can house several limited-use tools. Such tools are knee-grinders, layout machines, precision grinders, mid to large drill presses, vertical and horizontal milling machines, small lathes, etc. In fact, these types of tools may be "extra" to the modern plant due to the takeover by the new technology tool-machines. A perfect home for out-dated equipment is in or near a repair area. Usually, and this requires a check with the union representative, such tools are useful to the ordinary tool & die maker in the course of their everyday activity.

3.2.8   Time study the present crane situation and estimate the increased usage. In some situations that need more crane availability, a gantry or small bridge crane will suffice to take a measure of pressure from the main crane. Oftentimes, a survey will "discover" unused cranes. Some may have remained in a state of disrepair for so long a time that many may not consider them useable (or re-usable). Instead of a completely new crane installation, it could be more economical to invest in repairs for current equipment. Whatever the situation, the repair or replacement of cranes will depend on need and the ability to pay for the equipment. The "pay" is determined by the amount of "wait" time involved. If a trade person is forced to wait for a crane to disassemble a die, that time spent waiting is easily determined by considering the hourly rate of the person(s) involved and the cost per hour of the floor space used by the tool that is also waiting. The combined cost of "wait" times could easily justify the expense involved with updating the cranes. At least know the costs involved before making a reasonable judgement.

3.2.9 A wash station is included in this discussion of die PM as a reminder of the importance of cleanliness in the stamping operation. A wash station has major implications for stamping plant management. There are OSHA requirements and environmental concerns as well. Reclamation of costly chemicals, scrap and slug contamination, and waste treatment are only a few of the aspects considered when contemplating use of a steam booth. These are, surely, major expenses. However, there is nothing else that affects panel and the quality more than cleanliness. *It is the most important part of die PM.* Lint, slugs, slivers, dried dope not only directly affect panel quality, they indirectly affect panel quality by attacking the quality of the trim and flange line, the post and pad surfaces, and the mechanical on-die automation that contacts the panel. Wash every die, every time is the goal. The fact that it also improves employee morale is just a side-bar that will pay additional benefits.

3.2.10 A comprehensive die PM program will require a systematic replacement of wearable goods such as guide plates and pins/bushings. If not on a schedule, then dies should be, periodically, checked on a set-up plate for plate clearance not to exceed a pre-determined percentage of plate thickness. Sheet metal body panels may require as little as .007 opening to force replacement. Critical parts may be only .002 or .003. Hidden structural parts can get away with .010 clearance. Each facility must determine for itself what replacement criteria is necessary – depending on the methods employed and the parts produced. In any event, unless spare parts are available from suppliers immediately, there will be a need to store such parts at or near the repair areas. Cabinets or shelving is readily available from many different manufacturers. Again, consultation with trade people will determine the adequacy of any selection of storage equipment.

3.2.11 One valuable aspect of storage as it pertains to parts and especially dies is proximity. "Travel" time is just as valuable as "wait" time. Storing screws and plates and retainers and punches at a remote part of the plant my seem efficient and increase the ability to control inventory, but forcing employees to walk a distance to obtain parts and supplies will gobble up any perceived savings such a program is thought to provide. Travelling and needing assistance to bring a tool into the area for repair is another resource user that is avoided by providing floor space and equipment adjacent to the repair areas.

3.2.12 A plausible answer to the need for convenient, secure storage may be a vending machine. There are vendors providing this type of machine. Using company ID swipe cards, employees can come into the plant, gain entry to secure areas of the facility, use specialized equipment and "purchase" spare/replacement parts and supplies. Vending machines, periodically re-stocked by a route-person, is tailored to the specific area it serves and it can provide regularly used safety equipment such as glasses and ear plugs/muffs. In addition, it will allow better inventory control by recording part usage statistics. Maybe not THE answer but, certainly, one of the possible answers to the continuous improvement of the manufacturing process.

3.2.13 All of the foregoing exercises/topics, when properly considered and planned will result in a list that is compiled with an eye to expediting the PM program implementation at a particular facility. Each facility will have different needs. Each workforce will perceive those needs in their own way. Many are the ways to skin a cat comes to mind. The point is that items have been placed on the list for a reason. The reasons were validated by a common sense reckoning of cost-benefit analysis and identified by a measure of usefulness to determine purchase priority.

3.2.14 This is a valuable list. The next step is to purchase items on the list. When the workforce sees these items appear on the floor where they work, management's commitment to implement change and improve the system is validated. Unless the facility proposed for implementation of the die PM program is a very rare exception, hourly people will have seen many a program come and go without meaningful change because there is no meaningful support from management. The test of management's commitment is, and will ever remain, dependent on how much resource they provide to its implementation of any program.

3.3 Capture Floor Space

3.3.1   While it is not absolutely necessary, use of visible shop floor techniques will certainly enhance the credibility and usefulness of die maintenance areas. Defining floor spaces and installing equipment are important first-steps to take when expanding a "pilot" program to the entire stamping operation. Computers should be placed and dies given specific storage sites. Flow plans will help control traffic – vehicular and personnel. Identifying particular floor space is a positive method of launching a plant-wide die PM program.

3.3.2   The amount of space required by the die maintenance program is dictated by such factors as the die population and a reasonable forecast of future needs; the number of trade persons employed in the maintenance areas; how many shifts will work on the tools; die complexity; the load capacity of the press room; etc.

3.3.3   However much space is allocated will determine how many work cells are formed. The die maintenance area is a compilation of individual work cells, die storage sites, egress and ingress, and shared work centers. To maximize use of the available space, defining the areas with painted lines is almost a requirement. Leaving "spread" to the individual idiosyncrasies of each die maker will quickly eat up available space. Providing a planned layout, similar to the following drawing, will clearly direct the efficient use of available space.

See "PM Workcell Layout" in Appendix

3.3.4   Not only will die makers be limited as to where they can place die components, die setters, crane operators and such will have clear direction as to where they may place incoming tools and, by default reasoning, which dies to pick up and move to storage.

3.3.5   After defining these areas, the next step is to install the workbenches and ancillary equipment. Electrical outlets and air connections are standardized and similarly located from module to module. Benches, drawers and cabinet storage are provided in a consistent pattern. Work centers, complete with data entry computer stations, are uniformly equipped and evenly distributed throughout the entire maintenance area.

3.3.6   Die-specific storage sites should be established, and marked, adjacent to the maintenance areas. Marking identification numbers on the storage site will eliminate confusion and facilitate the compilation of a "map" that is used by die setters and die makers to quickly locate particular tools.

3.3.7   Natural progression will encourage another "visible plant floor" device. A physical "control board" is an easily produced aid to benefit the entire maintenance crew. Supervision may elect to assign specific tools to a specific maintenance team by posting the die to their work cell at the control board. The possibilities are endless and each refinement can mean a more efficient operation. Eventually, a control board can be the basic ingredient of a self-directed work force. It makes a lot of sense to begin such a move when implementing die PM since it is indicative of a more modern and efficient stamping operation. Each supporting component serves to strengthen the entire concept of modernization and efficiency.

3.3.8   Visible shop floor considerations are inclusive of every area and are used for every element of the stamping plant operation. If it is easier to locate dies when they are stored on a spot that shows its painted number or to drop off/pick up a tool at the (i.e.) red area of a work cell, and then it also makes sense to carry that pattern to other areas of the plant. Areas that affect the stamping operation and tooling in particular. "Dirty" and "clean" areas at the steam booth; "traffic in" and "traffic out" indicators at each end of the maintenance areas are additional examples of how the visible shop floor techniques can facilitate understanding and die movement at a stamping facility.

3.4   Code Structure

3.4.1   A system of codes is not essential to the successful implementation of a die PM program. However, a comprehensive coding system is **absolutely essential** to the long-term health of the entire stamping process. Bringing tools into the maintenance area for a systematic check of its components will provide a real benefit to the process. Identifying and recording every failure, PM activity and engineering change for every die will provide the basis for systematic improvement in the quality of the products made and the system that manufactured them. Capturing this data is best started as early as possible and is most efficiently done by use of codes.

3.4.2   Computers did not produce the paperless society that was promised. Actually, they seem to have increased paper use. That increase is due to the fact that many, many scenarios can be described based on the available data that has been entered into the computer. Every "what if…" produces more paper and another possible improvement to the system under study. What has really happened is that valuable minutia has been elevated to an extremely high level of prominence.

3.4.3   Computers are made to handle minutia. But, an understanding of how computers handle data will always bring one to realize that a short sequence of letters or numbers are more easily prepared for analysis than is an entire statement of several words. When several independent statements are the subject of analysis, by the computer, the task becomes impossible without rocket-science level design of the so-called software. A short sequence of letters or numbers is, basically, a code. Many repair-related activities are similar enough to group them and assign a code to the class. Then, when researching die performance, code x occurrences will reveal patterns of success or failure that are further investigated by viewing all statements associated with a particular tool.

3.4.4   Codes will indicate a broad picture with broad implications. These codes will, however, point to specific areas of concern or to specific tools. They will lead supervisors to further investigate repetitive problems. Certain codes will clearly point to probable design deficiencies. They will indicate inadequate repairs or sub-standard parts and supplies. Specific problems are located and codes used to identify likely repair methods. Basically, codes enable computer databases to more easily sort and identify specific features, fixes and faults associated with the tooling.

3.4.5   The accompanying code structure defines possible process faults. Every element of the stamping process is included so that every type of downtime is identified and assigned to a specific part of the process. The list can be used as is or it can be altered to reflect specific conditions at any manufacturing facility. The list is shown to indicate that a code can consist of letters that are arranged to quickly identify an area of operation and then to generally define what seems to have caused the fault or downtime.

3.4.6

See "Downtime Codes Example" in Appendix

3.4.7   Obviously, die repair is only a single component of this coding system. The prime factor is that capturing every incident of downtime and assigning it to the proper department is just as easy as capturing die problems alone. As was stated early-on in this book, die PM can drive improvements to every aspect of the stamping process. By gathering data such as shown here, improvements are identified for other departments as easily as for the die maintenance area. Properly coded minutia is also gathered and analyzed to provide substantial benefit to every part of the stamping process.

3.4.8   The ultimate goal of any process enhancement is complete compatibility with the manufacturing environment. This is accomplished with an intra-active workforce. Codes provide an opportunity to make the entire workforce aware of the goals and strategy of the die PM initiative. A representative from each trade and other classification should be invited to participate in a session where proper coding is discussed. It must be clear to all present that this activity is not about assigning blame but about discovering weaknesses, about solving problems, about improving the workplace environment for everyone.

3.4.9   The proof is determined by analyzing the numbers. The numbers are only available if they are collected. The collection starts on the pressroom floor and will only make sense if it is coded and stored on a database in a computer. The computer can be part of a huge corporate WAN or it can be a self-contained, off the shelf PC with a simple database software program. Whichever system is supported by the company in question, The software should be used on a daily basis to record data that is pertinent to the particular stamping process.

3.5 Downtime Codes

The first attack should focus on downtime. The workshop (if that is the format) should discover possible failures associated with each and every aspect of the stamping and material handling operation. These downtime codes are somewhat general in nature. DFS, for example, just determines that the problem concerns trim, flange or forming steels. There is no need to define the downtime any further. The real problem will be discovered later, by the trade person who repairs the fault. Later, when industry comes to fully realize the importance of PM, a set of standard location codes should be developed to provide an exact location of each problem.

3.6 Repair Codes

3.6.1   The second attack is more local in nature. Each trade or classification should generate a series of codes that will be designated as their repair codes. These codes will more accurately describe particular failures. For example, while a DFS will remain as the downtime code for analysis of the general performance of a die in the press room, the repair code will become the analysis code for the die repair areas. The repair codes are used to evaluate repairs, welding techniques, steel-coating durability, basic design flaws, process improvement, etc. Each classification has an opportunity to more closely define failures associated with their area of responsibility so that remedies are formulated and proper tools obtained. Probably the most important function regarding repair codes is that, properly analyzed, the data becomes the basis for future die design. Maybe the industry can finally avoid designing failure into the dies. The data obtained from proper repair coding will provide this opportunity. It will provide the feedback required by the TS16949-20XX.

3.7 Complexity

3.7.1   Assigning a complexity rating to dies really begs an industry standard method. Until that happens, the expertise of hourly and supervisory personnel should be employed to determine a level of complexity for every tool in the plant. This rating (or code) will assist supervision when assigning work to their team members. It will allow comptrollers to more accurately forecast maintenance costs associated with specific tooling. Rating dies will assist scheduling when they determine how many hours to allocate for PM and repair functions. When is a complexity 5 die that takes 12 hours x 2 people to completely disassemble, considered counter-productive to design and build in the emerging stamping environment of transfer presses and quick die changes? Six dies rated at 3 are maintained and die set a lot easier than five more complex dies are maintained and die set.

3.8   Assign Personnel

3.8.1   As the preparation for PM implementation continues, it will become apparent that a re-defining of job responsibilities is in order. The new definitions will pertain to both hourly and salary employees. Depending on the presence of a union and on any negotiated contract language, consultation with union representatives is a first step to ensure that the current descriptions are adequate insofar as the PM initiative is concerned. The intent should not be to create a new classification. The intent is to include PM responsibilities in any and all work practices.

3.9   Job Descriptions

3.9.1   Historically, even in unionized corporations with world-wide reach, job responsibilities for each trade and classification vary from plant to plant depending on the existing condition of the subject facility. This might suggest that there is significant latitude interpreting the contract language to include PM related exercises. In reality, for die makers, there is nothing required of them that does not fall within a normal interpretation of their usual job description.

3.9.2   Even if there is no issue relative to official job descriptions, the PM program is a distinct departure from past practice of the plant and special notice should be made of the newly required maintenance activity. In addition to an official posting of the PM responsibilities, supervisors are trained and prepared to relate the implications of the new program to each of their crew members. The main "implication" being the fact that PM is not a new program but a new way of life and that every crew member is responsible for PM. The simple truth is that a PM Crew should not exist. PM is a way of life and, as such, is a part of every person's daily routine.

3.9.3 The only sure way to encourage supervisory support for the PM initiative is to formulate performance goals that are PM related. Be emphatic. There are no PM Supervisors and there is no PM General Foremen. Each and every person who acts in a supervisory role must consider PM implications during the course of their work day. This important part of the work force must fully understand the depth of management's support and their resolute intent regarding the full implementation of a comprehensive tooling PM program.

3.10 Finalize Approach

3.10.1 Preparing for PM implementation is a daunting task. Knowing the names of the ducks is an important first step in getting all the ducks in a row. In addition to determining the size of each work team, each team is assigned a number of specific dies based on a quantity of complexity points. Performance measuring decisions must be implemented and data sources formalized with requests for daily updates. The records database structure must be finalized and tested to ensure complete capture of necessary information. To comply with TS16949-20XX requirements, procedures are developed concerning these new activities as well as system checks that ensure optimum implementation. A PM schedule can be produced and posted in the shop to announce the impending launch of the PM program. Comprehensive, generic checklists that were designed by the consensus of the trade people and supervisors who maintain them may be given a home, a central point where they are maintained in a database and made available to the die maintenance crew.

3.10.2 The PM office/coordinator is the sole provider of PM Checklist sheets. The work flow is more easily monitored by a single entity. So is tooling performance. The work team will come to know the procedures better that anyone else and their experience is conveyed to the PM office on a regular basis. However, all the elements are considered when evaluating the performance or each tool. Since the PM office receives copies of all shift-to-shift line-ups, production requirements, downtime reports and performance data, they are most aware of conditions that can and do affect the cycle-frequency decisions as they relate to checklist activities.

3.10.3 That is not to say that PM coordinators should ignore team member input. Rather, they should actively seek such input when making decisions about lengthening or shortening cycles between PM-based checklist activities.

3.10.4 To maintain agreement with the TS16949-20XX guidelines, a compliant procedure for each activity must be prepared and agreed to by all parties concerned. It is not a complicated process to prepare such documentation and it is best done at the outset of the PM program implementation. A compilation of all such procedures can form the basis of a training module that will ensure an understanding of the process as well as indicate the stepped expectations of management regarding adoption of a full PM schedule.

3.10.5 The most important question to be answered at program launch is: Where do I get the checklist? A reliable method must be discovered and implemented to ensure that every time a die enters the maintenance area, there is a checklist available for use by the trade people. Every facility has their own methods as well as myriad reasons for those methods. The main point to consider is that easy is always better than hard. Understanding that it is imperative that checklists are used to direct the PM of every tool, it follows that there is no excuse built into the system that allows the derelicts to ignore their responsibility. Checklists must be available in hard copy format. The PM Coordinator should maintain this process and provide for a timely checklist distribution.

3.11 Cycle Frequencies

3.11.1 Maintaining a PM schedule that is controlled by cycle frequencies can also be considered a time-based system. Delivery requirements are not controlled by "whenever we reach 5000 pieces" but by "send us 5000 pieces every 5 days". Therefore, it is an easy computation to arrive at the point when (probably) the cycle counts against a particular die or line of dies will reach 50,000 and require a visit to the maintenance area to perform the PM checklist procedure.

3.11.2 Tooling is created in a variety of forms and substance. The individual plant must use an educated guess to arrive at a starting point. Large body panel dies can start at 50,000 cycles. They are composed of hardened tool steel, iron and brass. Progressive dies may differ. Carbide inserts are more durable and that means longer runs – 100,000 or more at a time. Infrequent use may mean that a die is PM checked every time it is back from production. The Steering Committee should determine an appropriate level. They should also remember that the system is flexible and must adapt to experience. There should not be multiple levels of bureaucracy to decide when a change is needed in the target frequency.

3.12 Work Teams

3.12.1 The character of a PM program ultimately depends on the character of each plant. The same is true of the individual work team. If the tooling is large and complex, a minimum of two per shift are assigned to a team. Small simple dies that are easily handled can be tended by only one trade person per shift. The important thing to remember is that the "team" is composed of members from all three (or as many) shifts in the plant. Each member will eventually understand the proper method of communicating with their counterparts on their off-shifts. Communication, anticipation and mutual trust form the basis of a successful team effort.

3.12.2 There is an economy associated with proper assignment of work responsibilities and implied responsibility for specific equipment/ tooling. While the assignment of a specific bit of tooling to a specific trade person would seem to point a finger at that person whenever a failure occurs, there is wide support for just such a program. People in the skilled trades are proud people. Proud of their skill and proud of their more regarded position on the factory floor, They most commonly complain that they must clean up after someone else's "dirty work". The extra effort required for the successful implementation of a die PM program will come when trade people realize that whatever they do to and for "their" tooling will come back to them as increased failure or increased success – with the resultant effect on their self-imposed, day-to-day, work assignment.

3.12.3 The work teams will function most effectively when the individual members of the team become "experts" on specific tooling. The most reasonable method of assigning tools is by complexity rating (see above). Of course, a set of dies are best assigned to the same team (as opposed to each die being considered its own entity). The main purpose of retaining a die maker is to ensure productivity when the press line is in operation.

3.12.4 There are two approaches that can be considered. 1) hire an individual to trouble-shoot the dies that run on any particular press line or 2) allow team members to trouble-shoot the dies that are part of their regular work assignment, regardless of where they are run.

3.12.5 The easiest approach to assigning dies by complexity is to 1st) assign a complexity rating to each and every die, 2nd) add up the total points and then, 3rd) divide that total by the number of work teams. Finally, assign an (as near to) equal number of complexity points to each team – taking into consideration that, sometimes, entire sets of dies are assigned to each team, possibly causing an unequal assignment of points.

3.13 Database Structure

3.13.1 During the time leading up to the launch of the PM scheduled activities, the PM coordinator(s) should accumulate downtime data and record regular maintenance activities on the PM software. Hopefully, this activity will allow the PM coordinator to fine-tune the software being used as well as test the coding system that was developed by the Steering Committee. Inevitably, experience will require a change in the database structure to include additional information or it will require a change/addition to the developed code structure to better describe activities and failures that occur during the covered processes.

3.14 Data Sources

3.14.1   During the process of designing and preparing to launch the PM program, sources of data to support and evaluate program performance should have been identified and real data gathered. Managers should, at the point of program implementation, review the collected data and decide which data source(s) will best monitor the program. That is not to say that any other data will be ignored and discarded, it means that specific data will provide the measure of success or failure that is most meaningful to management. Continuous and complete data collection should remain a part of the manufacturing system. Without a doubt, process downtime is considered an important measure of program success.

3.14.2   How closely should downtime be calculated? Is it electronically determined – using the press control system to count the time? Within a minute? Or within 10 minutes? Obviously, the closer the better, but a particular plant may have issues that demand compromise. The main point is to begin tracking downtime and record into a database for later analysis

3.15 Order of Launch

3.15.1   Each work team should have input into construction of the PM schedule for their particular assignment of tools. Consideration is shown for the current reliability of the tools, Just In Time production considerations, available turn-around time and checklist content. Whatever the order that is finally determined; a complete, week-by-week schedule is generated, with every tool included, before the launch is effected.

3.15.2   A finalized PM schedule, based on cycle counts, is posted in each work cell and with supervisory and management personnel who have an interest in the stamping process. The posted schedule becomes an effective metric in and of itself. It also becomes an ongoing daily work-assignment for an essentially self-directed workforce that has accepted it as a stated goal requiring a determined effort to achieve.

3.15.3 The schedule can change whenever a destination assembly plant experiences a delay in production or when the final product experiences a downturn in sales. For these reasons, the schedule must remain somewhat flexible. It is a guide that may need adjusting from time to time. But, it is an important document that is used by the work team, supervision and management to control the maintenance process and improve the overall productivity of the production area.

3.15.4 To be sure, there was tremendous consternation during the preparation for WWII's D-Day. Success depended on the successful deployment of all available resources in a timely and effective manner. Equipment and personnel was collected and properly prepared for their individual assignment. Goals were set for every aspect of the operation and measures were established by which success – or failure – was determined. While the D-Day operation was of such a grand scale and of such grave importance as to dwarf anything attempted in a manufacturing facility, the basic elements of success are plainly shown and easy to understand. To be successful, a PM Steering Committee is smart to emulate the strategy used by the Allied Command to properly prepare themselves for the impending sea-change in the work culture of their facility.

3.16 Upgrade Tooling

3.16.1 An ideal launch of a comprehensive PM program would include the full rehabilitation of all tooling and capital equipment involved in the stamping process. That may or may not be possible. Whatever the case, a rehab is involved. The rehab phase of a PM launch provides an opportunity to not only evaluate the tools but also to document the tools. During the documentation process, the data is recorded in "blueprint booklets" (for lack of a better term), holes are identified and a chart prepared; metal-treatments areas are recorded; and purchased components are checked against the stock list for accuracy. This phase also allows the plant to properly re-weld all working edges. If there is any idea that quick die change is useful to the operation, rehab can include an effort to commonize shut heights.

3.16.2 Practicality demands that production continues unabated. Some parts can be over-produced to gain the time needed to tear down, document and rebuild the die. It is not always possible to do that in every case. The approach, then, is to take things a step at a time. The blank "blueprint booklet can guide the effort simply by virtue of what data has been recorded and what has not been recorded. Even if the rehab takes a month or two, it must be done.

3.16.3 For a die that started its life before PM, the cycle counting should begin immediately after the rehab is completed. Conversely, the count should begin immediately when a brand new die enters the population. This is not the time to give the die a look-see and a polish.

3.16.4 Rehab:

- Character lines;
- Trim edges;
- Flange lines;
- Replace gib/wear plates;
- Surface deficiencies;
- Lubrication lines;
- Air/nitro springs;
- Adapter/bolster plates;
- Clamping surfaces.
- Etc.

3.17 Blueprint Booklet

3.17.1 What does a booklet look like? It is utile. It is usable. Magazine articles and newspapers include lots of white space so that they are easy to read. Technical data and lists of parts don't have to be easy to read, but they should be easy to find. MS Excel provides the means to design a booklet on the cheap. A plus with this type of software is that almost anyone can use it and they are easily updated should the need arise.

3.17.2 It may seem that making a booklet for each and every die is overkill. It is not. In fact, it will become the most used document on the shop floor – especially when hole charts, shut heights, metal treatments and the like are included in the booklet. Of critical importance, though, is that changes are made on a timely basis. Whenever engineering changes are made, the die is (usually) altered. If these changes to the booklet data take weeks and months to accomplish, the trades people will lose confidence in management's commitment to the project. Lose that and the program will lose support (as another management boondoggle) and eventually fail.

3.17.3   One of the handiest documents that can be made available to the trades people and their supervisors is the hole chart. Simply put, the hole chart is a part print with numerical call-outs for each and every hole. The call-outs are listed along with additional information that describes the dimensional tolerances and the use of the hole. It avoids undue concern for drain holes and ensures that critical mating holes are not dismissed out of hand as unimportant. Even though each die is accompanied by a conventional stock list, it is a safe bet that the purchasing department has little awareness of the total holes involved in the stamping/assembly process. That means they don't have a clue regarding the need/replacement ratio that will guide them when they stock the crib. The activity involved with preparing hole charts will provide this information which is essential to the efficient operation of the stamping process.

3.17.4   While gathering the data to fill the blueprint booklets, it is easy to also identify and record every instance (location) of special metal treatment. Chrome-plating, ion-nitriding and the like are important and costly enhancements to the durability and formability aspects of the treated dies. They require special procedures to repair or polish the surfaces. What happens when that area is changed by the engineers? What performance standards are used to evaluate the application of the treatment? What justifies the expense?

3.17.5   Improvement of the maintenance process is a matter of doing things and then rating their effectiveness – the results. The evaluation process starts by identifying and recording a lot of information and continues by collecting data pertinent to the process. Finally, the data is analyzed so that intelligent enhancements are made to the tooling to increase its reliability. In other words, metal treatments are not evaluated unless and until they are identified and recorded in an appropriate medium (the database of the PM program). This is one of the "valuable minutias" (pg. 79) mentioned earlier that can add value to the PM program and therefore improve the overall maintenance program.

3.17.6 A meaningful measure of the PM program's success is not achieved unless and until the tooling is returned to an original specification. As previously stated, the rehabilitation can take many weeks before its so-called "launch" into the PM program. Damaged trim edges and worn flange surfaces will never be as good as original. However, "close" may be close enough. To come "close", it is required that any improperly welded areas are ground away and re-welded according to accepted standards – complete with pre-heat and post-heat. Surprisingly, many maintenance crews are unaware or unable to properly weld damaged die steels during the normal course of the workday. Welding is a primary cause of downtime failures related to tooling. When a plant begins to collect data related to downtime, coded entries reflecting burrs and tears or distortion will soon reveal the extent of damage done to tooling with improperly welded repairs.

3.17.7 Many times, especially during the construction of large body panel dies, some components are substituted for those listed on the formal stock list. Some are done conveniently and others are the result of changes being drawn on the part print after the change is made to the tooling. It doesn't matter why or how, all that matters is that real components are recorded and the design source is made aware of the accurate stock list so that their records will coincide with the condition of the tooling.

3.17.8 The engineers may also react if they find that what was designed to punch an 8mm hole is now punching a 25mm hole into a post that is now weakened with a slug hole that is three times as large as planned. Happens all the time. "Problem" dies are not usually designed by inept engineers. They are the result of a lack of communication between the engineering function and the production/maintenance function. The first step to resolving this potential problem is to gather and check information using the Blueprint Booklet.

3.17.9 Record shut heights. Because Quick Die Change (QDC) depends on accuracy and consistency, some of the principles of QDC can apply to PM practices. One of the essential elements of QDC is a common shut height for all dies running in a press or press line. The reason that this practice is beneficial is because it further reduces the opportunity for damage when press rams are raised and lowered to accommodate the various heights of every die. In fact, engineering should be encouraged to design the tooling based on common shut heights of dies going in to the same press (es).

3.18 Train Staff

3.18.1 One of the more important activities to consider when preparing for the launch of a comprehensive tooling PM program is the training of members of the plant staff. In this context, training means that these managers are provided with the long term goals and their effect on the productivity of the facility's stamping operation. The current state of operation must also be presented, in brutal truth fashion, so that all are aware of the scope of the problems and the need for an appropriate remedy. This knowledge will better assist staff members when they decide on which goals to seek. The goals are, then, more easily converted and adjusted for every level of supervision that answers to the managers on staff.

3.18.2 It behooves the PM Coordinator and the PM Champion to provide a list of reasonable expectations along an adjustable time-line of implementation. Thus, when staff members sign on to support this project, they have a road map that they can easily follow and one from which they can evaluate the progress of the PM project.

Emphasis must be placed on control mechanisms for every aspect of tooling maintenance. Equipment is a consideration, but people are more so. The biggest problem is the big "excuse": "we've been doing it that way for xx years". Strangely enough, the supervisors can provide production throughput; scrap reduction; reduced work hours; etc; etc. They provide these things because they are important to their boss and their boss demands that they comply with these certain directives. The deal is sealed when management makes an initiative part of the supervisor's annual review. No play, no pay. Works every time. The point is that goals are formulated that are easily measured and quickly made part of the annual review process.

3.18.4   Immediately following the training program for staff members, the program should launch. Admittedly, staff members probably have a long attention span. But, to build credibility and support for the PM initiative, things should happen almost immediately. The sooner things begin, the sooner those results will bolster the over-all program.

3.18.5   With this in mind, a reasonable time line (TL) should be provided to managers. The TL should show the stepped implementation by including one production area after another; by dedicating more and more of the workforce to PM centered maintenance; by acquiring/ rebuilding more and more equipment for use in the maintenance areas; and by achieving significant productivity goals in a timely manner. It is also necessary to provide points upon that TL where reviews occur and where quantitative goals are reached.

3.18.6   It should be a perfunctory action, but acquiring the support of every member of staff is critical. Even one enemy or skeptic can hobble the program. Obviously, results can pretty well overcome any objection. However, fighting with a manager diverts attention from the critical issue at hand. Namely, a smooth and orderly launch of a sea-change in the way business is conducted.

3.19. Current State

3.19.1   It is a relatively easy task to use the newly-created downtime codes, or similar tool, to determine the current state of disrepair for all tooling being used at a stamping facility. Since the coding system is prepared early-on in the preparation for launch, it is implemented immediately and used to form a baseline from which to measure success or failure. Every metric that is deemed useful for evaluation is allowed to gather data prior to program launch. Sometimes, a worthy production control scheduling software is a source for relevant data. In short, determine the number of monthly downtime hours that result from tooling-related problems; how much of a stockpile feathers the "nest-egg" of shippable parts; what is the throughput per day on any given production line. Any and all of these measures will provide a current state picture.

3.19.2 Hourly employees are where the rubber meets the road. Care should be taken to properly explain what the PM initiative is all about and what role each employee is expected to employ that will improve corporate viability and expansion in the marketplace. Workshops/training sessions are planned to develop and distribute common procedures, explain the use of checklists and codes, and encourage feedback. Managers must express whole-hearted support for PM centered maintenance that will result in direct (individual) responsibility for tooling maintenance. Those responsibilities will include an understanding of root-cause analysis principles, cycle frequency rationale and the benefits of a self-directed workforce.

3.19.3 Because the change in operating procedures is so great, management (staff) must express their support for the changes taking place in the plant. Hourly employees expect leadership from the managers and will usually respond with enthusiasm to any change that: 1) includes their input; 2) improves the product; 3) makes their work life easier. These people know the process better than anyone else and can bring about the needed changes faster than anyone else. It is management's job to gain their support and confidence and lead the way.

3.19.4 The first opportunity to involve hourly employees is through a workshop setting. In a workshop, their brains are picked to determine such things as: the one right procedure for picking up/dropping off a die; reporting techniques; what coding structure is best to report failure or repair; maintenance module requirements; etc. Many companies have already defined some procedures to comply with TS16949-20XX requirements. Direct interaction with hourly workers will further refine those procedures and, possibly, discover new opportunities for establishing a common approach to workplace activity.

3.19.5 The importance of using coded entries in today's computer-enabled society cannot be understated. Most, if not all, enterprise resource planning/production management software consists of a very sophisticated database application. The reason is that data is entered, or acquired, and then analyzed to more effectively form and execute the business plan. Databases store data. They sort and compare data for analysis. It is almost impossible to sort long-hand information.

3.19.6 i.e.: How can long-hand entries possibly gather together statements such as: "the die section chipped at the corner and caused a burr on the panel"; and "a chipped section is responsible for a burr on the bracket"? These statements pretty much mean the same thing and describe the same condition. But, a database cannot efficiently sort them from similar statements and count them as two incidents of failure. Properly described as DBR, for example, the two incidents become identical and are sorted, counted and prepared for management review.

3.19.7 Coded entries do not eliminate long-hand entries. A description of a problem with specific language is a valuable tool. It is valuable when seeking an answer to a specific problem with a specific tool. An audit of a tool is such an example. However, evaluating a program or discovering common failures requires data that is accumulated across many tools and, sometimes, many departments. Coded entries are accurate, concise, descriptive and easily used. The codes for an entire plant can be contained on one sheet of paper and available for use by anyone who is responsible for maintaining a tool, entering data into a database or reporting the daily incidents of failure and repair to managers, supervisors and trades people.

3.20 Root Cause Codes

3.20.1 To properly manage a tooling PM program, it is necessary to use two distinct types of codes. First is the "failure" or downtime code which reports every incident of failure during the production process. A root cause or "repair" code is used when describing the real reason for the failure, that discovery process is performed by the trade person when they take apart the tool and see what caused the failure. This is not a formal root cause analysis but it is a hands-on discovery process that is more easily reported with a coded entry. Because it is a more detailed description of a problem, it needs more digits and, possibly, more fields to hold the entire code. Because these codes are more complicated, extra care is taken to describe their use to the trades.

3.20.2 Hourly employees are expected to provide the all-important feedback to the PM coordinator's office. Fine-tuning the checklist requires that observations are attached to completed checklists. "No wear – looks good" might mean that an activity is placed on a longer-interval list. "Pretty galled – dressed up a little" would indicate a move to a shorter interval. It might be an expected response from an employee (to give pertinent feedback) but nothing is left to chance. The training period is the most opportune time to emphasize the need and, then, direct every employee to submit recommendations and encourage comments pertaining to expediting the PM program by improvement of each checklist.

3.20.3 Checklist "fatigue" is addressed during the training period. Why do grown-ups have to mark down everything they do and turn in a piece of paper as proof of their cooperation? Why is everything documented? These are common objections ands are best answered with facts. The simple overriding fact is that TS16949-20XX requires documentation. The practical answer is that the most important use for checklists is that they provide the means to evaluate the process and the aforementioned, inscribed comments can guide the continuous improvement efforts for the tool. Interestingly, the checklist empowers the hourly person to direct the efforts of the facility, as a whole, to improve the production process.

3.20.1 The best place to start with development of custom checklists is with a generic checklist. A list of activities that are concerned with the general makeup of a type of die can direct most of the activity. Engineering changes, quality improvements, die elimination have an impact on the makeup of a custom checklist. Change is inevitable and it must begin with the first use of a generic list. "Check bolts on sub-plate for tight" does not appear on a checklist for a die that has no sub-plate. "Check flange steel for galling" would be an important addition to a list for a pierce die with a minor flange feature. It could be somewhat hidden, after all. "Scratch out" this or "add" that are normal inscriptions on a new checklist.

3.21 New Equipment

3.21.1   After a survey to determine the best use of investment dollars to support the maintenance operation, the requested equipment is purchased and installed prior to launch of the PM program. Most likely, the manufacturer of a machine will offer training for a designated operator so that the equipment is properly operated and its features fully used and appreciated. Why is everyone else denied this opportunity to learn how to run a machine? Maximum use should equal maximum benefit to the company. Too often, equipment stands idle because there is a lack of training. Too frequently, damage is inflicted by those who are unfamiliar with how things work. Proper use and proper care, as opposed to idle and broke, should provide the currency to justify an on-going training program for new and transferred employees who operate capital equipment.

3.22 Data Flow

3.22.1   Data is like blood. It is necessary to maintaining the activity. If a data source is constricted or clogged, data will not find its way to the point where it is a benefit to the process. Stop the flow to and from any specific portion of the process and that portion will weaken and fail, ultimately crippling the entire process. As mentioned earlier in the text, information is on paper, data are on the computer. Information is read. Data are analyzed.

3.22.2   At the training stage, it is important to stress the importance of clear and specific information that will support the maintenance of any specific tool. It is also important that information is not a substitute for data. Information is used by the trade person as a guide when working on a tool. It is more economical that information is retained as a hard-copy resource – eliminating the need for computer use by hourly personnel. Data, however, are analyzed and are available to anyone with any interest in the production process. The training program should make clear the purpose of accurate information and the data it generates so that hourly people will respect their vital role in its gathering.

3.22.3 Phony fears that documenting time and activities will endanger their job security is just that: phony. Of course, supervisory personnel must be held in check and prevented from using PM documented information to discipline any member of the workforce. This is not an option. If the trade people are disciplined by a supervisor who uses such data in this way, the supervisor should be discharged immediately. The PM program will fail if the workforce fears retaliation from supervision based on data collected by the workers themselves. No one is so stupid that they will provide the means for their own discipline to management.

3.22.4 Data are fed into a computer. Computers use data to provide innumerable tools that will support a thorough analysis of the tools and processes surrounding an efficient production program. By providing hourly workers with a set of codes that describe situations relative to their responsibility within the overall process, they are encouraged to simplify their descriptions and provide succinct reports. Simple descriptions and succinct reports will serve to expedite the data entry process, reducing the need for personnel committed to PM support activities.

3.22.5 Trained to understand the principles of PM-centered maintenance; equipped with the tools to support their maintenance activities; armed with analysis and information to guide their efforts: what better tools are needed to support a self-directed workforce? The shared analysis is sufficient to maintain control of the entire program. Proper data collection and analysis will point all the fingers necessary to identify failure while suggesting corrective measures to resolve any problem.

3.22.6 Trade people can be assigned to care for specific tools. They are then responsible for engineering changes, repairs, trouble-shooting the tool during production and for performing checklist activities to meet PM cycle requirements. Many companies understand the value of assigning specific people to resolve problems associated with a specific source or product. Why is there no value in assigning specific people to each tool or process? Rated tools (by complexity) provide the means to equalize the work load. Tool performance will provide the motivation to execute quality fixes, accurate changes and thorough

PM checklist procedures. It is the answer to an efficient and effective tool maintenance program.

3.23 Construct Work Cells

3.23.1 The concept of work cells may have more to do with 5S and similar systems of workplace management than with a PM initiative. However, making a change as drastic as PM-centered maintenance depends on other aspects of the work environment changing as well. Work cell design; centrally located machine tools, placement of commonly used tools/equipment, air/power outlets, tool storage, work bench availability; computer access; die movement strategies and 5S activities: all have an impact on the overall success of the program. The training period allows the PM coordinator and the champion to educate the hourly and supervisory workforce concerning the physical changes that will take place in the plant. It is also an opportunity for feedback from these folks that may strengthen the program with minor changes.

3.23.2 Every plant may have the need to alter this design to suit particular conditions. The main point is that enough space is allocated to each cell so that the trade person has room to work and to open the die. This cell may be a single one placed near a production area or it may be one of a cluster of cells that are placed around a common area that houses small machine tools or similar equipment.

See "PM Workcell Layout" in Appendix.

3.23.3 The object of having work cells is to expedite the maintenance function by making it easier for a trade person to access tools and equipment that they need to perform their job. Easier, of course, means faster too. With this idea in mind, placing machine tools in close proximity to a cell makes sense as well. Depending upon shop practice and union contract – if any – small machine tools would include a variety of grinders, a CMM, a small boring mill, a Bridgeport-type mill, a small drill press, a cut-off saw, etc. Of course, everything should be analyzed from a cost-benefit point of view. The word of caution that is operative here is real cost versus real benefit. It is easy to say no. Try to say yes. If the analysis won't support the purchase or relocation of such equipment, then don't do it. Experience dictates that it should.

3.23.4 Die separators, portable magnetic drilling equipment, portable difraccto machines, carts, portable tool boxes, etc. should be located in central areas that are easily accessible from all other areas of the plant. Not only does this discipline provide a more organized look to the work area, it also saves hours of hunting for the elusive equipment that is needed every day by the conscientious trade person.

3.23.5 Make sure that the maintenance crew is apprised of the program launch date so that they can install sufficient air outlets and electrical outlets to support each tooling maintenance work cell.

3.23.6 Whether stored in a sophisticated auto-racking system or placed on the plant floor, it will save time and effort if every tool has a specific "home". If a guide book does not direct anyone to the proper storage site of a particular die, then it is not an adequate system and requires improvement. PM will save production time. It doesn't make sense to lose that time when hunting for a die to set, machine or to repair in any way.

3.23.7 If every employee is expected to produce the same amount of work in a day, then each should have the same amount of resources at their disposal. Many times, the most common resource is often the least available. The bad habit is that locks go onto drawers whenever someone leaves employ. The bad result is that newer, and sometimes older, employees are subject to working in sub-standard conditions. Storage drawers and cabinets are appropriated to each trade person in equal quantity and condition. Therefore, a work cell design should include bench work space, a cabinet or drawer for each skilled worker, space for two tool boxes (rough and precision), a substantial vise, a small, ground plate (for small set-up activities), a compressed air source and electrical outlets.

3.23.8 All elements of the 5S discipline support a proactive PM centered maintenance initiative. In particular, smart placement and specific locations refer to work cell design and implementation. Painting lines on the floor will identify the work cell boundaries, the drop-off and pick-up area as well as locate the specific cell to anyone else in the plant. Hand in hand with Visual Factory Management (VFM), 5S will allow for an intelligent transition to a self-directed workforce.

3.23.9 Not only does VFM help to define the best layout of the factory floor, it also provides for communication between labor and management, shift to shift, and department to department. Construction of a board with hooks and disks is an easy method to organize the work flow and instruct members of the workforce. This is just one of many common-sense approaches to the management of today's factory floor.

3.23.10 Die Status Board

Work Flow Management

Cell

1	o
2	o
3	o
4	
5	o
6	

```
o o o o o o o o    o o
o o o o   o o o o o o
o o o o o o   o o o o o o o o
o   o   o o o o   o
```

Press Room Assignments

o	o	o	o	o	o
P1	P2	P3	P4	P5	P6

o	CMM
o o	Die Set
o o	Die Wash
	Drill Press
o	Mill
	Tryout

o = disc with embossed die #

Work Flow Management

3.23.11 Too often, factory managers will err when they decide to provide too few cranes to support the maintenance function. A usable crane is not an employee benefit. Its purchase is based on a cost-benefit analysis that seeks justification from lost hours/minutes experienced when an employee is forced to wait to use a crane to lift a heavy object. Sometimes, the building cannot support a sufficient number of cranes to serve the work loads. Gantry cranes may be preferable since they share the load with the floor – providing less stress on the building walls. Crane manufacturers will provide all the analysis needed to solve difficult situations that require the use of a crane.

3.23.12 Since most people are at least aware of how a computer functions, it is not unexpected that workers can enter data relating to their workday. To accomplish this function, enough computers are placed around the shop floor to facilitate data entry and data retrieval by anyone and everyone. The cost to purchase and maintain such a system will determine whether to employ a full time clerk to perform these tasks. The important consideration is that trade people have quick access to as much information and data as they need to maintain their dies.

3.24. Locate Storage

3.24.1 Whether using a sophisticated stack-storage system or merely placing dies on the floor, an organized approach beats haphazard every time. Use VFM principles and visually identify every storage space with a die number. (The same goes for specialized automation equipment). Allocated space is determined with safety in mind. That means that walkways are provided if using the floor as storage and, of course, using a crane requires less space than using a fork-lift. Finding space is no easy task. One plant, with which the author is familiar, enjoyed the services of an industrial engineer for three months to identify and design such a storage space. And it wasn't overkill.

3.24.2 Storage is a partner of the die set operation since this team handles the tooling far more than any other. Establishing a procedure for moving dies to a specific storage spot might be governed by a series of tags that can be affixed to the tool. One tag for repair, a tag for maintenance and so on. These tags are the responsibility of a trade person or a supervisor. The main point is that nothing moves without a tag and that the location of every tool is known at all times.

3.25 Install Equipment

3.25.1 Pilot programs and test areas are developed and experimented with to ensure effectiveness. However, when the final step is taken to mainstream PM-centered maintenance, it is important that everything is in place and functioning. Installing equipment means that machine tools are bolted in place and functional; portable equipment is delivered, set up and operating; work cells are identified and properly outfitted; cranes and handling equipment is installed and meets safety requirements; computers and support software are installed and de-bugged; and that communication devices are ready for use.

3.26 Launch

3.26.1 The Champion and the Steering Committee are identified and appointed to their position. The Steering Committee has identified codes and equipment needs. Floor space and storage space has been captured and made ready for use by the maintenance crew; baseline data has been collected and stored on computer software; hourly and staff personnel are trained; work cells are ready and waiting; support machines have been purchased, installed and operating. There is nothing left to do but LAUNCH.

3.26.2 In limited situations with a small workforce, imposition of the fiat works well. The boss decides what to do, develops a checklist from an intimate knowledge of the tooling, decides on a workable cycle-based PM schedule and assigns people to perform the PM activity. Whatever approach will work will achieve impressive results. Deterioration of the tools does not care if the facility covers many acres or a street corner; employs four thousand or only four people; has thirty-five press lines or only one. Tools respond to care and maintenance and react with reliability and quality improvement. The degree to which it responds is determined by management's level of commitment and involvement in the process

3.26.3 Everyone has a part to play. The trades perform the PM tasks; the PM Team enters data and works to improve the process; supervision works to expedite the process at every juncture; management facilitates the process by removing roadblocks. For this effort, everyone benefits as well. The trades are relieved from the more stressful reactive maintenance mode; supervision can add quality and productivity to the process without being "cops"; management can more accurately forecast budgets and re-claim floor space for added profit centers. All can experience the warm glow of a more secure future that profitability provides.

4. Systems Support

4.1 Definitions

To be completely successful, preventive maintenance (PM) must enjoy the cooperation and wholehearted support of every person in the stamping plant. In the final analysis, PM-centered maintenance is not a program as much as it is an operating system, a way to successfully conduct business, if you will. For purposes of this chapter, Systems Support means cooperation and support from the plant manager, comptroller, production managers, maintenance, engineering, I/S professionals, machinists, purchasing department, welders and tool and die makers. The role each must play in the day-to-day operation of the plant is explained:

Plant Manager The plant manager/owner is the most important person when it comes to support of the PM initiative. Whoever decides to approach this person with hopes of beginning a PM-centered die maintenance program must properly prepare themselves. Accurate data is critical. Return to the discussion in chapter one to properly evaluate the cost of the present process.

Comptroller Gaining the support of the company/plant comptroller can be a daunting task. But, after the plant manager, the comptroller is the most important person to have on board and actively participating with the PM initiative. The PM champion would do well to consider this part of the groundwork as a worthwhile challenge.

Production Manager If anyone should support a tooling PM program, it is the production manager. A successful PM program will ensure greater reliability during production; a higher threshold of product quality; a reduction in scrap production; better manpower utilization; and a greater opportunity to utilize newer stamping processes.

Champion   The key player in this labor-management relationship called tooling PM is the Champion. This person should be a manager (as opposed to a supervisor) with responsibilities at the superintendent level of authority. Depending on the plant custom, this level would be able to purchase needed equipment and supplies as well as send PM committee members for PM-specific training. Of primary importance is their belief that tooling PM will serve to enhance the quality and increase the productivity of the press room.

Maintenance Dept.   The role that the maintenance department plays in a tooling PM program is extremely important. In addition to their responsibility for making sure that the heat, lights and water will work, they concern themselves with all capital operating equipment. By initiating their own PM program, they can help ensure the success of the tooling program by providing important feedback relative to failure and reliability issues that directly affect their equipment.

Engineering   Design improvement can be a significant goal of the tooling PM program – a long-term goal, but one that is attainable as well as capable of providing significant reward to the production process. Just the inherent process of maintaining records is a valuable commodity that can help engineers to stop designing failure into the tooling. The impact of different materials; component parts; complex die design; and steel properties are just a few of the areas that can be enriched with the data that rolls off the die PM program.

I/S Professionals   Since computers play a basic role in a comprehensive tooling PM program, the role played by the information service department is a crucial one. By monitoring the progress of the PM program, I/S can make decisions about the appropriate and timely proliferation of computers onto the shop floor. They can develop hierarchical access and guide the customization of the software as the PM process develops and data acquisition becomes more specialized. With a broad understanding of the capabilities inherent to a comprehensive tooling PM process as well as the intent to evolve into a predictive maintenance program and, finally, into a total productive maintenance system, I/S can plan the installation of LANs and corporate intranet components such that progress will not be hindered by lack of systems hardware and support.

Tool Machines   The tooling PM program is designed to improve the tooling maintenance function, it only stands to reason that expediting the process is desirable as well. The most productive step that can be taken is to form tool-machine centers that truly serve the needs of the trade people who maintain the tooling. Just the exercise of investigating machine tools will be beneficial. New technology will have a significant impact on maintenance and machining functions. Computer driven, 5-axis machining centers can be used in a variety of money-saving ways to enhance operations. Die separators and portable Diffracto machines can also improve the maintenance function. Of course, the simple drill, saw, surface grinder and Bridgeport-type machine need to be in ample supply.

Tool Crib   Replacement parts and hand tools are the province of the tool crib. It is folly to think that tool maintenance can be improved without considering the ability of the tool crib to supply adequate numbers of replacement parts. It doesn't matter whether the crib can be electronically accessed through a company-wide intra-net or physically accessed by presenting a verbal request at the call window. What matters is that the parts are available and that usage is closely tracked.

Welding   Minor repair of tool steels necessitates the use of the welding process. The primary concern is that a process is used that will provide proper heat-treating both before and after the weld is applied. Production requirements must be flexible enough to accommodate proper weld procedures.

Skilled Trades   The people identified as skilled trade workers provide the backbone of any PM program. The toolmaker and the diemaker service tooling, therefore their input is essential when designing the PM program and their support is crucial to the success of tooling PM. Trade people will clarify the damage and the repair mode, provide written reports on daily progress and will, with proper training and sufficient equipment support, expedite the stamping process.

PM Coordinator   The PM Coordinator is the most important player in a PM implementation. Even the PM Champion is part of the supporting cast. The day-to-day activities that become a comprehensive

PM process are directed — if not designed — by the PM Coordinator. They can even be an hourly trade person as long as they enjoy the full support of management as well as the people they work with. The PM Coordinator should also have enough skills to operate a computer and use common software packages. Hopefully, they will possess some writing ability so that they can effectively communicate with everyone concerned.

4.2 What's In It For Me?

4.2.1 Now, a more complete discussion of everyone's role is in order. This material will include responsibilities and rewards for everyone concerned. There will be warnings and cautions as well as strong prompts and suggested courses of action.

4.3 Plant Manager

4.3.1 Generally, the top executive in the plant is not easily swayed with vague and grandiose claims of failure or projected success. Their view is the long view, a view that is probably based on mostly financial concerns. Presenting the collected facts should be enough to gain their attention. The size of the wound (from which the cost of failure flows) should then be enough to motivate this person to endorse a comprehensive program that ensures/improves reliability and quality.

4.3.2 That endorsement must include the selection of an appropriate champion – one who enjoys the confidence of the plant manager. The champion must be someone who is trusted and one who is willing, if necessary, to make drastic changes and who will spend money wisely. Implementing PM will virtually eliminate the status quo and it may include some transfer of power to hourly personnel.

4.3.3 This "endorsement" also includes the introduction of PM related criteria for annual reviews that determine the compensation made available to managers and supervisory personnel. It is critical that the by-products of PM – quality and reliability – replace production quotas as measurables during the annual review process of supervisory job performance.

4.3.4   To ensure the continued support of the plant manager, their metrics must be included in the process of selecting the metrics by which the program is measured. At least one chart should be of their own design, one that tracks data especially significant to them. They must have confidence in the PM Champion and the PM Coordinator. Regular charts and reports will help maintain that critical confidence and support.

4.3.5   From a Plant Manager's point of view, a successful, properly run tooling PM program will yield specific benefits:

- Process reliability – dies should work, presses should run.
- Consistent product quality – clean and sharp dies make fewer burrs and mars under a regular maintenance schedule.
- Updated technology – reliability allows for purchase of newer, better presses because re-capture of capital expenditure is more quickly recovered when unplanned downtime is eliminated.
- Space for new products – reliability reduces the need for excessive part storage, releasing floor space for other use.
- Increased profit – consistent product quality eliminates re-work and scrap.

4.4   Comptroller

4.4.1   Comptrollers are chiefly concerned with the financial success of an enterprise. They rely on data and details and viability. Satisfying this requirement will provide the Champion and the PM Coordinator with enough knowledge to become confident in the endeavor and proficient in its defense and implementation.

4.4.2   The comptroller should be asking for specific data and, although projected, reasonable goals that reflect a fiscally viable activity that enhances the financial bottom line for the company. To that end, the people responsible for implementing a comprehensive tooling PM initiative should develop and disperse their accumulated data to the plant manager and comptroller in the form of budgets, cost-benefit analysis, safety concerns and manpower utilization. They should expect the comptroller to ask for more or refined elements of data that refer to their specific areas of concern.

4.4.3   The process of winning over the comptroller will begin with a request to provide the actual cost per square foot of specific areas of the facility. The cost of an idle production area, parts storage areas, re-work stations, scrap, are all specific concerns that will be help evaluate the need for, and the success of, a comprehensive tooling PM program.

4.4.4   The comptroller will provide resources based on the initial request of the plant manager. They can untangle the process by anticipating requests that logically flow from a process with which they have become familiar and fully interactive. Again, that familiarity will only come with frequent meetings and updates from the PM Coordinator and Champion.

4.4.5   After full PM implementation, the ensuing years of process improvement will provide, with the interaction of a competent comptroller:

- Accurate expectations of maintenance costs for new and existing products.
- Benefits that help planning activities related to manpower and training.
- A firmer grasp of budgeting relative to new product production processes.

4.4.6   These specific benefits should encourage the comptroller to enthusiastically embrace the PM initiative by their early and consistent interaction with PM.

4.5   Production Manager

4.5.1   During the production process, trim steels become dull and chip. They produce burrs and slivers while demanding a greater effort from the press to accomplish its mission. Flanges gall and tear the metal – making more debris. More debris causes more damage and more galls and burrs. Most likely, this process results in a loss of product quality and decreased productivity due to the frequent, prolonged stops needed to make minor repairs to the resident die/tool. Left to achieve the extreme, dies are destroyed by neglect.

4.5.2 Of course, production managers don't care if a die is destroyed. They need enough parts to fulfill their commitment to the customer and will sacrifice anything, at the moment, to meet that obligation. The benefit of a comprehensive tooling PM program is that reliability and quality are its direct by-products and nothing material must be sacrificed to meet production standards.

4.5.3 Acceptable quality means different things to different people and different circumstances. <u>It should mean</u> that every part is made to specification. Period.

4.5.3.1 In most cases, when the process is completely out of control, just getting a form into the sheet metal is sufficient. Hand work takes care of the rest because the customer needs the parts and it's cheaper to hand finish the parts than it is to pay for a factory shutdown. A laborer with a file can stand at the end of the production line and make up for poor maintenance procedures. It is amazing how little quality is needed to produce acceptable parts. Then, when someone underbids the job, there is wonderment that they can possibly make money. Incremental failure creeps in the back door and debilitates the entire workforce.

4.5.3.2 If the production manager is promised that every part will be made to specification, they will become an avid supporter of the PM program for tooling. However, the empty promise must be filled with concrete results in very short order.

4.5.4 A natural result of a successful PM process is the virtual elimination of scrap. A properly maintained die does not pull burrs, split nor deform panels. The problem does not disappear overnight but a consistent application of PM activity will provide a "no-scrap" dividend within only a few die sets.

4.5.5 It may be debatable whether manpower reductions can be achieved simply by improving throughput, reliability and quality. But, when coupled with the ability to employ newer stamping and transfer technologies, there is no question. At least, trouble shooters can be re-assigned and quality control people can cover a wider area of responsibility. The re-work artists and their area can be reduced. Scrap handlers can be retired as well as the hilo drivers who serve their needs.

4.5.6   The most exciting changes in the production manager's area may come from the ability to use newer equipment. Equipment designed for modern manufacturing processes. Transfer presses, automatic racking systems, tandem presses fed by robotic arms: all such wonders are useable when the tooling is reliably producing panels that meet the customer's specification without die-related downtime.

4.5.7   Persistent failure during a stamping production run is both costly and frustrating. Production workers, in a (heretofore) traditional operation, act as watchful eyes to detect dings, dents, tears, coins, burrs, etc. Sometimes, they inadvertently cause damage just by handling the panel as they move it from one press to the next. It is costly to stop this type of line for a quick fix of a chipped trim section. It is even more costly to stop a tandem press, replete with the entire loaded transfer apparatus, to make such an adjustment. Spending millions of dollars to closely watch panels for defects is not a good idea. In fact, it probably doesn't make sense to most manufacturers.

4.5.8   The obvious remedy to stop and start stamping and the short road to employment of new press technology is a proven, comprehensive, tooling PM program. The 5 – 9 - 12 production workers that are assigned to each line of conventional presses can be re-assigned to the transfer press profit centers that are made possible by PM. Preventive Maintenance also makes possible a conversion of the stamping plant to a "Just-In-Time" manufacturer that doesn't have to appropriate acres of plant floor space to "backup panel" storage.

4.5.9   As stated earlier, the Production Manager has the most to gain from a comprehensive tooling PM program:

- Reallocated manpower – better use of productive hands making other parts instead of repairing sub-standard parts made with sub-standard tools.

- New technology – stop and start production makes it impossible to utilize faster, more efficient presses.
- Consistent quality – every part made to specification.
- Just-In-Time – a promise instead of a dream.

4.6 Champion

4.6.1 The first inclination when selecting a 'champion" for a new program introduction is to select an up-and-comer who wants to prove him or herself. In this instance, that may be a good idea since the older, more experienced manager is more likely to resist change. Plus, they have learned to work the system and compose reports that support the stretch-goals contained in their annual review guidelines. They may not be as comfortable collecting and analyzing data that directs their daily, weekly, monthly activities.

4.6.2 However, the younger manager may lack an important ingredient: experience. Experience may not have a great effect when associated with a new concept such as tooling PM. But, it provides currency when that younger manager asks for support from other managers. Of course, having the full support of the plant manager, who selected them to serve as champion, will usually overcome objections from the negative side and ensure at least minimal cooperation from the entire management team.

4.6.3 Don't get this wrong. Enthusiastic support by all involved is the best way to ensure a successful implementation of tooling PM practices. The reality, though, is that there may be skepticism regarding this new idea and some brute force may be necessary to establish a foothold-type demonstration area or pilot program that will serve to prove the PM concept before full implementation. It is for this reason that the Champion must have sufficient influence and ability to provide all the ingredients for a credible pilot.

4.6.4 The Champion can implement drastic change in very short order by changing the way supervision is graded and compensated. Annual review criteria, for PM to achieve full implementation, must include PM oriented goals. Criteria can include such things as:

checklists completed; downtime reduction; number of tools included in the program after rehab; etc. Proper weighting of these items will also increase their importance to the supervisory personnel – ensuring compliance and support.

4.6.5   Early on in the process, the Champion should avail themself of basic training in the disciplines that support equipment PM in the manufacturing environment. The real benefit of this training will come to the fore when the principles of Total Productive Maintenance or Reliability Centered Maintenance provide the connection between all maintenance activity in the plant and the bottom-line improvements that will be realized under such proven programs.

4.6.5.1 Early in the process, the Champion should also send PM Committee members to PM-specific training. The entire team must work to improve the PM program and they will only do so if they all understand the concept, the supporting technologies and the metrics that will be used to evaluate their efforts to improve the process under their control.

4.6.6   There is no room for a CYA individual. Supervision (general foremen and supervisors) are unlikely prospects for the role of Champion. By definition, they are too short term in their outlook. They are concerned with daily production quotas and immediate quality fixes to answer customer concerns and complaints.

4.6.7   Since tooling quality is at the mercy of equipment quality, and vice versa, the Champion must work to obtain the cooperation of any and all departments which "touch" stamping and tooling. Most people are "peer" responsive. Therefore, the Champion must gain the support of each manager of each department. This will ensure that each will implement similar PM oriented goals for the supervisors under their authority. Then, all employees will be aware of management's expectations and goals regarding quality and productivity standards that are supported by the PM initiative.

4.6.8   Since PM will change the way business is conducted, there may be different needs on the shop floor. It is best to seek these improvements and prepare for them. The needs will be new because the tooling will be better maintained and fewer failures will occur. With fewer failures, there will be more time available for quality enhancement exercises such as panel surface improvement, replacement of standard wear details, etc. By the way, it is more cost-effective to replace a worn wear plate than it is to grind and shim it. So, keeping a supply of plates is important. They should be ordered by numbers and quantities recorded in the "Blueprint Booklets". The Champion can expedite the process by informing the Purchasing Department of the need for an open purchase order for this specific purpose.

4.6.9   By getting the money to support the PM program with purchases of supplies and equipment, by getting the people to participate with enthusiasm in a comprehensive tooling PM program, the Champion will get the results they need to improve product quality and productivity. That will support their annual employment review.

4.7   Maintenance

4.7.1   A primary function of the maintenance department, relative to die PM, is code-development cooperation. Since data drives PM, it is very important that failures are properly identified and applied. Each department can benefit from this process since data is data. Only the code identifies the source of a problem. It only makes sense to capture all downtime data, assign appropriate codes and then allow each department to use the data to drive their own maintenance activities.

4.7.2   there is no need for discourse here about the value of equipment PM. Virtually all manufacturing-related trade magazines provide information relative to the need for this type of vigilant maintenance that ensures a more efficient plant operation. What needs to be emphasized, though, is that PM is a way of life and it is all inclusive in nature. Good dies are destroyed by bad presses. Good presses are destroyed by bad dies. Machine tools must be properly maintained if they are to consistently make replacement parts for tooling. Improper handling and improper storage also wreaks havoc with tooling.

4.7.3   An equipment PM process will ensure proper operation of all press and related machinery. The supporting documentation will provide the means to evaluate performance and direct on-going efforts to improve plant operation. In addition, most software programs that support equipment PM can be modified to also support tooling PM – keeping all PM-related data stored in and accessible from the same system.

4.7.4   When equipment is maintained with a comprehensive PM-oriented process, any failure is more easily assigned to a specific cause. When that cause is determined to be tooling-related, the pertinent information can then be offered to the tooling support area so that they can effect repairs or improve their design to maximize efficiency and minimize failure.

4.7.5   Tonnage monitors or thermographic systems can measure variations sufficiently enough to provide data relative to the operation of a single die. More pressure or greater heat generation can indicate die failure. Such data would help indicate a maintenance requirement for tools that operate within any particular press. The data is there to be used. It only has to be accessed and properly analyzed.

4.7   Engineering

4.7.1   Engineering is the obvious choice to document the PM process and track its progress. They can provide an oversight to the PM team that will ensure compliance with the planned implementation of a comprehensive tooling PM program. Engineering can also develop procedures that, properly documented, will comply with quality systems such as TS16949-20XX et al.

4.7.2   The foundation of the PM process has to be data. Watching the process operate and recording its success and failure on a daily basis will generate the necessary data. There was much space accorded to explaining the design of the downtime/failure code structure and the repair codes too. The payoff is in their use. Simple, understandable codes are the key to swift and accurate analysis. Longhand explanations – properly recorded against a particular tool – provide the means to determine the cause of each failure, such as a weak structural design. The coding systems provide the means to identify recurring problems experienced by many tools, such as a damaged press or incorrect spray lubricant. The entire body of data is a valuable resource to the entire stamping process. The engineer is the one who should appreciate it most.

4.7.3   The consistent use of failure codes and repair codes can provide the engineering staff with the opportunity to evaluate each tool. For example: compare dies that produce similar parts but are made from different components. Is machine steel a better investment than cast iron? Do composite guide plates perform as well as solid brass or steel? What weld rod does a better job of repairing a composite section? or a post section? These and similar questions can be answered. The regular reviews inherent in a comprehensive PM program are often enough to provide meaningful data for analyses by members of the engineering staff.

4.7.4   Because the PM process requires the disassembly of the tooling, special attention should be paid to the time required to take things apart during a routine inspection. Taking apart a die with two lower slides and a collapsing post on the lower shoe and an aerial cam affixed to the upper shoe certainly takes more time than a simpler no/one cam die. The difference in time has a dollar value that should be evaluated to determine the advisability to design such dies in the future.

4.7.5   Newer transfer presses are eliminating a great deal of the material handling requirements as well as providing the means to set a larger number of smaller dies on the moving bolsters. There is no need to fight progress. Sometimes, dies can be simplified and made easier to work on. Hard, cold, accurate data should be the means to determine whether or not to combine operations or to separate them for maximum efficiency.

4.7.6   Steel is the main ingredient in most stamping processes. Nowadays, it is commonplace to select steel from a menu, prototype the performance and customize its final composition to ensure optimum performance. In-plant steel laboratories, jointly funded by supplier and the end-user, are commonplace commodities that pay considerable dividends to savvy stampers.

4.7.7   Properly recorded and coded failures will point an accusing finger at steel variation in a relatively short time span. Splits, tears, coins, etc. will quickly accumulate when material is at fault – provided that the tool itself is under the control of a comprehensive tooling PM program. The point being that improving steel composition is extremely difficult to accomplish if steel is not the only variable in a sample run. PM can remove die failure as a process variable.

4.8   Information Services

4.8.1   The I/S department should be involved with the PM program from the very beginning. By understanding the ultimate goal of the program, they can make a better decision regarding software development.

4.8.2   There is some benefit to the purchase of existing software in that report formats are already developed. Database fields already interact with one another where appropriate. The most important though, is that a software company will, thanks to the profit motive, continually update and upgrade the package or "engine" upon which the application is based. Most companies will customize their software to meet individual needs. They charge fees for this, of course, but that fee may prove more affordable for a small to mid-size company than the expense associated with building a custom application from the ground up. To be sure, custom is better but "off the shelf" is better than not at all.

4.8.3   As early as possible, computer terminals should be placed within easy access of the trades people who perform maintenance on the resident tooling. The I/S department should plan to train these employees on proper use of the developed software. It is important that there is a general understanding of the failure codes and of the repair codes. Most importantly, they must understand that the coded entries will be used to quickly identify failures for analysis while their commentaries will be used to exactly describe problems that might be systemic and possible to avoid when future tooling is designed. When this understanding is achieved, there should be little problem obtaining accurate input by hourly personnel.

4.8.4   Unfortunately, I/S can easily be used as a code-word for paranoia. Intricate levels of security protected by ever-changing passwords and input monitoring will quickly bring data input to a halt. Most employees will not abide this type of control. They will expect easy access – just like at home – and a friendly graphic interface. If the experience is not comfortable for them, they will quickly abandon that part of the process. The idea is to make and keep the people on the shop floor happily inputting data to support the critical analysis necessary for a successful PM program. It is not necessary to keep the I/S people happy at the expense of the overall process.

4.8.5   If there is data that does not concern the hourly employee, it should not appear on their screen. If it does concern them, it should be plainly labeled and clearly displayed – with a printout option. Periodic surveys will discover their perceptions of software shortcomings and desired enhancements. If the changes will help them perform their job more effectively and more efficiently, that is a dollar value to the company that can be measured against the cost to provide the enhancement. Simply then, it's a dollar and cents decision.

4.8.6   With a comprehensive PM package, pressroom failures will be recorded with codes, downtime, scrap costs, etc. This type of information should be available to supervisory personnel so that they can properly assign and direct the workforce. In an environment where hourly personnel are self-directed, this type of data should be made available to them as well. Supervisors will also benefit from access to reports that indicate an accumulation of failures. Similar failures of similar dies in the same press may indicate a press-related problem. Similar failures of welded repairs might indicate an inappropriate composition of a welding rod, encouraging the search for a replacement. They should be able to generate reports and assign work from their terminal. They should not be able to change existing documents.

4.8.7   Typically, a manager should have access to the same information that is available to a supervisor. Most likely, they will be directed to view the data as a result of a prompt from a supervisor who needs direction or wants support for a plan of corrective action. Periodic viewing of charts and performance data will allow the manager to be kept abreast of the beneficial impact of the PM program implementation. This data will also support requests for capital expenditures and program enhancements.

4.8.8   The software and computerized maintenance system belongs to the two primary PM operatives in the plant. They must have access to every level of the software program since their job is to direct activity that will enhance the over-all PM-centered maintenance process. The collected data will benefit the many areas of plant operation and should be of great interest to staff members and managers in each department. However, it will probably be the Champion or PM Coordinator who presents data to these people and indicates how it will help each department/area prosper in a competitive manufacturing environment.

4.8.9   The Champion and PM Coordinator and the I/S department personnel have a mutual responsibility to work closely together as they perfect the software and find ways to utilize the collected data. Indeed, the need for additional, different data may arise and cause a change in the graphic interface and database structure. A quick implementation of such a change will enhance the credibility of the die PM initiative and provide appropriate service to the aforementioned data-users who ultimately benefit from careful analysis of existing stamping conditions.

4.9   Machines

4.9.1   Modern technology makes machine replacement almost unavoidable. Unfortunately, the up-front expense of purchasing suitable machine tools places them out of reach to many small stamping operations. Tactics such as digitized details for rapid replacement provides the backbone of tool readiness. Rapid replacement of inserts and details is essential when faced with the prospect of supporting an idle multi-million dollar transfer press operation.

4.9.2   Depending on the size of the manufacturing facility, one or more machine centers should be established for the exclusive use of resident trade people. Simple math can justify the expense of such centers. Average "wait time" x cost per employee per hour = amount of money available (currently being wasted) to purchase equipment.

4.9.3   A currently-running machine, that is operated by a dedicated trade person, may be less than state of the art. Using this "found money" (previous paragraph), the business can purchase a new machine that provides new features and capabilities and the older machine can be re-located to a machining center for use by the die maintenance crew to accomplish quick repairs and adjustments. Not only will this approach save money (fewer steps; faster response to quality shutdowns; quicker repairs; etc.) it will make money by allowing exploitation of the state of the art capabilities of the equipment. The plant's entire approach to maintenance can change to take advantage of the increasingly CAD-CAM oriented world of stamping/manufacturing.

4.9.4   Replacing a shaper, vertical mill and a horizontal mill with a 5-axis machine can significantly benefit the maintenance operation. Electronically stored tool-paths provide the ability to reproduce critical die steels in a matter of hours, if not minutes. Re-machining welded components back to original datum is a snap. There is no real need to delve into the benefits of modern machining centers. The point is that these dream machines are a required component of any manufacturing facility and, for some, embracing a comprehensive tooling PM program will provide the finances as well as the financial incentive to acquire the equipment as painlessly as possible while making the day to day activity even more efficient.

4.9.5   With the current availability of die separating machines, there is no valid reason to take die sets apart any other way. Any sane person should cringe in horror whenever a pry bar is brought in close proximity to a die. Use of a crane and chains or hooks will inevitably result, sooner or later, in a clinched die. Pounding the die together for another try or prying it apart with a crowbar, will inflict damage – sometimes small; likely significant; sometimes catastrophic.

4.9.5.1 These hydraulic units will open or close a die without event and in very short order and without danger of damage. There are a number of manufacturers who make this equipment. One should be available to the trade person in every machine center that supports die maintenance.

4.9.6 Diffracto™ is a trade name, but it denotes a machine that can highlight surface irregularities on a die post of a draw die. A portable unit can be rolled up to a die and used to assist the trade person in eliminating panel irregularities caused by the inconsistent surface of a die post or pad. What is invisible to the naked eye and a "light house" is readily apparent on the screen of a Diffraccto machine. It is an important piece of equipment that should be available for daily use by trouble-shooting die makers.

4.9.7 Drills, saws, grinders are usually in plentiful supply around a die maintenance shop. Mention of them is made to remind the reader of the basics. It is not uncommon that basics are forgotten when a far-reaching and process-altering program such as PM is being implemented. Don't forget!

4.10 Tool Crib

4.10.1 It is extremely important for the purchasing department to fully support tooling maintenance with an adequate supply of replacement parts. The beginning of a tooling PM program is an optimal time to modernize purchasing operations so that usage data can become part of the available data that is used to analyze tool performance as well as process reliability.

4.10.2 Although it is not a primary concern from the vantage point of the intent of this book, it bears notation that cribs are rarely placed in close proximity to anything, let alone everything. How much does it add to the cost of a $4.50 punch to include the time wasted by walking to the crib and back to pick it up? When the press is stopped and production workers are waiting?

4.10.3 Newly (fairly) available technology introduces the possibility of placing vending machines in close proximity to stamping presses. Electronically enhanced data can be available that shows when and how many (for example) punches were obtained, what job number to charge, and whether to order a new supply or not. Each machine can be used to vend – at the swipe of an employee ID card – products that pertain to specific dies that run in specific presses.

4.10.4 If 1000, .250" punches are in use plant-wide, it may not be worthwhile knowing that 15 are replaced each day. However, if 14 of them are being replaced in the same die at the same physical location each day, then there is great cause for concern. The use of electronics and computer-generated reports will identify situations such as this with relative ease. These same reports can help identify sub-standard replacement parts and the company that manufactured them. Cost comparisons can be quickly made between products of different manufacturers as to durability and quantity purchase levels.

4.10.5 There is also a subtle insinuation that certain practices are not cost-effective – if cost figures are included as part of the view screen. For example, cutting down a .250 punch blank (cost $4.50) to .188 ($4.50 + use of an OD grinder and an operator's time) is, clearly, not a wise decision.

4.11 Welding

4.11.1 The constraints of a tight production schedule will sometimes necessitate a quick repair. The goal of achieving a production standard, at the expense of the tooling, is fool's gold. However, the plant culture is the real enemy and the culprit is the management review criteria. If production count is primary, supervisors will turn to the "hot shear" to save their day.

4.11.2 The "hot shear" occurs when there is an occurrence of a chipped/damaged cutting steel that leaves a no-go burr on the sheet metal panel. The damaged steel is welded in the press. The press is turned on, the weld heated to cherry red and the press is turned over and the steel is "repaired" with a quick stroke of the press and a quick re-sharpening of the welded area. Works like a charm! However, this process degrades the cutter and the disintegration of the steel is inevitable.

4.11.3 While the "hot shear" is, hopefully, an uncommon activity, the normal repair process may increase the need for this destructive practice. Chips and cracks that are identified during the repair and maintenance activities, if they are improperly welded, will become candidates for a "hot shear" in the very near future. If the normal repair is not properly pre-heated, welded and post-heated, then – again – the steel degrades and it becomes a candidate for failure.

4.11.4 The process is always the solution. An efficient process is one that is monitored and, possibly, electronically controlled. Many times, the post-heat part of the process is the one that suffers. Probably because it is a step-down regimen and requires more equipment than one oven set at one temperature. More than one oven means more capital expenditure. A bank of ovens outfitted with electronic controls means a lot more expenditure.

4.11.4.1 Justification for this type of investment depends on need. Need depends on reliability and reliability depends on quality tooling. Once again, the cost of process downtime will come into play. This failure expense will provide the cost-savings computation to justify, or not, an investment in a proper, on-site welding process.

4.12 Skilled Trades

4.12.1 Early on, the resident skilled trade person is needed to help compile the codes for failure identification. These codes provide the basis for downtime analysis and repair procedure development.

4.12.2 The PM process has little value if it cannot be analyzed and quantified. Perceived value only goes so far, actual value – displayed as factual data complete with applied costing – is needed to compel the support of management's staff officers. These people control the dollars that will enable the PM initiative. They should see real cost savings as well as continued process improvement. Staff officers understand that reliability will free up floor space to increase the square footage that is committed to productive enterprise. Codes enable quick and accurate analysis of the stamping operation as tooling reliability impacts the stamping operation.

4.12.3 Bringing the skilled trade worker up to date on a regular basis is a wonderful idea. However, it is a concept that hardly ever reaches fruition. That reality is a mystery. The modern skilled trade person earns more money than the average Ph.D. Skilled-trades persons are of above average intellect and resident experts and educators in their chosen field train them for almost four years. These people are a valuable resource that are under-exploited by managers who seem to dismiss them as mere "factory rats".

4.13 "Training"

4.13.1 Training consists of letting capable workers know that management wants to improve results in their specific area of responsibility; that there is a plan; and that they have specific responsibilities that will impact its successful implementation. After all, a successful PM process will minimize their time spent under the ram of a press making quick-fix repairs. It will ensure their long-term employment by increasing the fiscal health of the company for whom they work. And, it will improve their work environment while evening the workload. "Training" will not make up for abusive treatment nor sub-standard wages.

4.14 Records

4.14.1 Necessary to any process, are records of completion that can be used as history and as guides for continuous improvement practices. If PM check sheets are used to document, analyze and improve the process, they will be readily used by the trade person as they work in support of management's long-term goals. If PM check sheets are used by supervision in the disciplinary process to rate individual performance, they will be quickly abandoned – and it won't matter whether the shop is unionized or not.

4.14.2 It is smart to begin with a generic check sheet for each tool. Instruct the trade person to identify components that may not be listed as well as eliminate unnecessary steps. Quick and accurate response to their suggestions will enhance process credibility and support among the primary system users. It will also seamlessly create a fully customized library of individual check sheets.

4.14.3 In a production setting, as well as in the repair shop, a hole chart is a very valuable commodity. Simply put, it is a drawing of the part with call-outs for every punched, pierced and lanced hole. Manufacturer's numbers should be added to properly identify the perishable tool (punch and button) and facilitate the ordering/replacement process. Identifying the purpose of the hole allows for possible leeway in emergency replacement techniques (drainage holes may allow variance while pilot holes may not).

4.14.4   As previously stated, the Blueprint Booklet is utile. It is filled with pertinent information. It is updated in a very timely manner and all the (controlled) copies are kept current as well. MS Excel, used to design the booklet, is a plus since almost anyone can use it and these documents are easily updated. They will become the most used document on the shop floor – especially when hole charts, shut heights, metal treatments and the like are included in the booklet. It is extremely important that they are continually reviewed and updated. If changes to the booklet data take weeks and months to accomplish, management's commitment to the project will be questioned. If the trade people lose confidence in management's commitment, the program will lose support (as another management boondoggle) and surely fail.

4.14.5   A suitable database has already been discussed. To satisfy the requirements of TS16949-20XX and similar quality assurance standards, record keeping should be fairly simple. Binders and file cabinets can be used. Depending on the cycle frequency of the PM process, all check sheets up to and including the major review point (say 500K hits) can be kept together in a binder (a large binder with dividers can be used to contain sheets for several tools). After the 500K review, and a decision is made to increase/maintain/reduce frequency, the sheets for a particular tool should be moved to a file folder. That file should be kept until the tool passes out of the system (plant).

4.14.6   Usually, design staff will use the electronic files to identify problematic tool design. However, when they identify a problem, the paper records will be used to research the actual problem and identify a plausible solution. TS16949-20XX also requires a record keeping strategy that is used to provide "feedback" to the assorted levels of any manufacturing enterprise. These requirements should be embraced and used to build a strong die maintenance program.

4.15 Equipment

4.15.1 Equipment that was previously identified as useful to expedite tooling repair and maintenance must be maintained. Ideally, it too must be properly maintained in a process that includes preventive maintenance techniques.

4.15.2 In addition, technology upgrades should be a regular item in the plant budget. Most major manufacturers of tool machines and equipment will gladly provide the cost-savings to be expected by implementing the technology contained in their new and improved tool machine. Since the cost of downtime has already been determined, it seems a simple matter to determine whether or not an upgrade can be cost-effective or not.

4.16 TPM

4.16.1 Total Productive Maintenance is one form of discipline to guide the manufacturing industry toward increased profit through process control. Why is it kept secret from the front line troops in this war on waste? The vast majority of working people want to be productive. They lose heart when their efforts go for naught; when scrap is the result of their efforts.

4.17 Seven S

4.17.1 In the author's stamping plant, the Seven S discipline was quickly embraced and enforced by hourly personnel even while it was disregarded by supervision. Fortunately, managers decisively confronted the issues and emphatically supported the Seven S protocol. They required supervisory participation by quickly adding 7S compliance to the annual review criteria of every supervisory-level employee. Proactive management is a critical ingredient that will ensure the success of a comprehensive tooling preventive maintenance program.

4.18 PM Coordinator

4.18.1 Every major component of the plant workforce should have a PM Coordinator: tooling; equipment; administrative; systems support;

etc.. The needs of each individual facility will determine the total number of coordinators required to support the plant's operation and the plant's productivity.

4.18.2. Consider the coordinator as the most important person on the floor. They must be willing to stick their neck out and make changes, as they are needed, to continuously improve the PM implementation. It does not matter whether they are hourly, salary, supervisory or managerial personnel. What matters most is that they are committed to the program and that they answer to the PM Champion who will take the case for PM directly to the plant manager and the plant staff.

4.18.3 Initially, the PM Coordinator will be responsible for identifying codes (previous chapter). They will guide the creation of appropriate data that will be baselines for measuring program effectiveness. As each tool (die) is refurbished, the PM Coordinator will prepare a file that contains the blueprint booklet, the hole charts, checklists, PM schedules, etc. As more tools are added, pertinent charts can be designed that will visually display the burgeoning benefits derived from a more in-control process. The PM Coordinator, on the front line, will address the needs of the supporting trades people.

4.18.4 Finally, as the PM program develops, the PM Coordinator must make regular detailed reports to Staff concerning the needs and benefits derived from current efforts to implement a comprehensive PM program. These periodic reports will be the basis for them to develop a relationship with each member of Staff. This relationship will facilitate the implementation of a Total Productive Maintenance process when the proper time comes. Staff awareness of program effectiveness will also remove the untimely roadblocks that seem to spring up and derail the best efforts of all concerned.

4.19 Summary

Although the PM Coordinator and the PM Champion are primary enablers in the implementation of a comprehensive tooling PM program, every person in the plant has an impact on the quality of the final outcome. Implementation should not be kept secret from employees. For sure, there will be skepticism and uncertainties. Every new "boondoggle" from management is treated with contempt. Until. Until there is clear evidence that management will support and promote this effort and until management adopts it's principles as standard operating procedure. That is why measurement is critical to success. There must be an improvement of the fundamental culture of the environment. Collected data supported with planning, followed by certain, successful execution of a remedy is not only attainable but it is also more attainable when plant personnel accept and support PM principles. Measured progress is the key that unlocks process improvement.

5. Predictive Maintenance

5.1 Definitions

Predictive Maintenance (PdM): is the skillful use of technology to identify potential failure and, then, schedule adjustments to the process during regular maintenance intervals.

PdM for Tooling: With the use of technology, downtime and loss of quality to the manufactured product is avoided while maintaining a high level of throughput. PdM relies on an effective and mature preventive maintenance (PM) program.

Systematic, comprehensive checking - and subsequent adjustment - of tools and dies will eventually allow a maintenance program to reach a threshold where substantial improvements are no longer available without the use of some electronic device(s).

5.2 Basic needs

5.2.1 PdM relies as much on a mature PM program as it does on technology. A mature PM program ensures that there is sufficient collected data on which to base a decision to advance PM to PdM. Clearly, PdM does not replace PM. It builds on PM so that the manufacturer is able to avoid catastrophic failure, thereby increasing uptime and system reliability.

5.2.2 Mean time to repair and mean time between failures will be reduced while every instance of failure is recorded. Checklists, after numerous tool reviews (at 500K hits or more), are completely customized to each tool and they are recorded in a computerized maintenance management system. This system provides the means to evaluate the effectiveness of the resident PM process and directs a continuing process improvement while it helps avoid process deterioration.

5.2.3 What is left to consider is whether enough improvement is available to help pay for PdM and its inherent costs (i.e.: cost of electronics, manpower, equipment, etc.). And, there is limited technology available. Only two companies manufacture pertinent electronics that can be adapted to provide true PdM for tooling application.

5.3 Technology

5.3.1 The relevant and available technologies to provide PdM capabilities are very few and far between. Right now, there is one device that is, for all intents and purposes, a load monitor. It should work. Worn details should increase the load reading while a broken detail – say, a punch – will decrease the required load. Another device reads sound waves and is quite accurate when properly used. The trick with both devices is experience.

5.3.2 The only way to benefit from the use of these devices is to experience failure. The accumulated failures will provide the data that is needed to interpret the readings and set the acceptable parameters. The sound that a galled form steel makes must be identified. A dull pierce punch needs how much extra force to do its job? Will the technology be used to identify failure – like a broken pierce punch – or will it be used to show potential for failure – like a galled form steel?

5.3.3 In addition to sound waves and load monitoring, PdM techniques that protect equipment include: infrared cameras; vibration sensors; tribology; and ultra-sonic listening devices. Probably, each of these technologies, save tribology, can be adapted to provide a warning of impending failure for tooling applications. Wider use of these technologies will provide the answer. But, before there is a need for these devices, the industry must become more PM conscious. The entire stamping industry must mature relative to tooling maintenance.

5.3.4 Contact organizations such as the following to gain knowledge and insight into PdM technologies:

- Infraspection Institute (support@infraspection.com)

- Vibration Institute (vibinst@anet-chi.com)
- Maintenance & Reliability Center, Univ. of Tenn. (mrc@ utk.edu)
- PdMA Corporation (813) 621-6463

5.3.5   These organizations are involved in some aspect of the predictive maintenance field. They either host or participate in regional or national conferences that treat PdM as a way of life, a culture. Until tooling PM is more universally accepted, the basics of PM and PdM have to be learned from the equipment side of the house. Fortunately, a successful tooling PM program requires an equipment PM program. If a facility has neither, they should develop side by side. Whatever the case, the principles – the mindset – must be learned and adapted to benefit tooling if a manufacturer expects to reap the full benefits of a comprehensive tooling maintenance program.

5.4   Collected Data

5.4.1   The time to begin collecting performance data is right now. Do not wait until this book is read and discussed and a basic plan is formulated. Begin gathering information immediately. What information? Any information and all information, as much information as can be stored in a computerized maintenance management system (CMMS). It is important that such a system can be customized and periodically changed to keep up with an evolving PM program. It is almost impossible to know exactly what data may have value in the future. If it is collected, it is available. Collecting many bits of information is as easy as collecting one bit of information.

5.4.2   There is a lot of maintenance software (CMMS) available today. All of it is equipment oriented and some of it can be customized to meet the needs of a tooling PM operation. There are caveats to consider.

5.4.3   Equipment PM is activity oriented, period. The main focus is completing each activity at specific intervals. Checklists for tooling PM are also activity oriented. But, with tooling PM, the most important activities to record are the small failures that occur during the actual stamping activity. Small failures are actually quality concerns like burrs, tears, splits, dings, dents and missing holes.

```
┌─────────────────────────────────────────────────────────────────────┐
│                                                                       │
│                        Die Record                                     │
│                                                                       │
│    Log No.:   111      Date:                     Accume Count:  12345 │
│                                                                       │
│       Die No.:   A123       Operation: Trim        Priority: A        │
│    Description:   Front Fender                                         │
│    Department:   Die Maintenance Repair Area 03                       │
│    Home Press:   22A                                                  │
│                                                                       │
│                     Function  Code       Description                  │
│                      Primary:   8   Miscellaneous Activity            │
│              Effect on Parts:  11   Preventive Maintenance Cycle      │
│          Specific Component:   48   250K Cycle Checklist              │
│             "X" Axis Location:  000  Entire Die                       │
│             "Y" Axis Location:  000  Entire Die                       │
│                                                                       │
│            Trouble Code: DPM  Preventive Maintenance Procedure        │
│                                                                       │
└─────────────────────────────────────────────────────────────────────┘
```

Die Record

5.4.4   There are no small failures with equipment. Either the press runs or it doesn't. Lots of granddaddy crashes have occurred because some supervisor had to get the panel count up to standard before shutting down an ailing transfer press for repair. Bypassing safety, shutdown equipment seems to be a regular practice in stamping plants with a culture that requires meeting panel counts "or else".

5.4.5   It's not so easy with sheet metal panels. Quality concerns have to be addressed in a timely manner or, literally, thousands of miscreant panels will require fixing before they will be acceptable to the client assembly operation. Tooling PM is, therefore, charged with avoiding these quality failures by continuous attention to trim edges, flange steels, guidance components, automation fixtures, etc. In short, the die is judged by what it makes as opposed to how well it opens and closes.

5.4.6   CMMS software, as it comes in the box, may not be sufficient for use as tooling PM control software. The manufacturer should be willing to customize it. The final product must be able to store recorded data for hundreds of dies/tooling; specifically sort the data and assign downtime and repair time per incident of failure; sort by coded entry;

and accume the time and associated costs for evaluation on a periodic basis; and, finally, allow for explanatory text input that provides the details concerning each incident.

5.4.7   The CMMS is the foundation on which a PdM program is launched. Unlike equipment, each tool is absolutely unique. Data is gathered from birth and goes away when a tool is scrapped. PdM for equipment like motors and pumps and relays, etc. can be based on industry-wide experience. A GE 100 hp motor can be rated against every one of thousands produced by the manufacturer with likelihood that the data is relevant. A hydraulic pump and system operates like any other pump made by the same manufacturer. The hydraulic oil can be analyzed to identify suspended particulants and compared to the oil from thousands of similar pumps. Electrical boxes and relays and breakers are standard in industrial use. Infrared cameras can be used to compare their condition to each and every other such device made by the manufacturer. In tooling, history is like an autobiography, relatively short-lived and a different story for each tool. That is why it is essential that data be collected as early as possible in the life of the tool. This "keystone" data is what will be compared to later performance data of the tool to verify its condition.

5.4.8   Even though the data collection goal is to record every bit of production data, the die PM team should focus on the data relevant to their process. In-press repairs and those accomplished in the repair shop are equally important. True, those causing downtime are much more costly. However, recording each repair is required. Whenever a PM checklist is completed (it could take a few shifts) the date and the total hours spent should be recorded. Even the engineering change should be tracked. It may be considered continuous improvement but it also will affect die performance. It will be valuable information to know that productivity went south following completion of a specific engineering change and that a specific "fix" cured the resultant problem. There are three letter codes for each of these types of data and there are five-position numerical designations to describe (loosely termed) root causes. Using codes makes the evaluation process much more efficient and they facilitate the data collection that provides the basis for any type of predictive maintenance effort.

5.4.9.1 Because every die has a unique PM checklist, it is not necessary to record every checked activity every time. Simply recording that the checklist was completed is sufficient. The numeric code will identify the level of the PM check (i.e.: 50K hits; 250K hits; etc.). Adding the time to complete will prove useful when evaluating the entire program against downtime and repair costs.

5.4.9.2 Any problem identified during a PM checklist activity is considered a repair situation and the time needed to rectify the problem is entered as repair time. Dressing a sharp trim edge or removing the onset of galling from a form steel is not. Repairing a cracked weld is.

5.4.9.3 The PM checklist is, primarily, a communication device. It will indicate the items that must be checked at a specific cycle count and, it allows the die maker to provide feedback to the PM coordinator concerning the condition of the die. An engineering change may have added or deleted components that do not currently appear on the checklist. A checked item may not show any discernable degree of wear and earn an upgrade from the 50k cycle check to the 100k cycle check – reducing the time spent on a 50k cycle check.

5.4.9.4 Suggestions that are concerned with checklist activities, as well as any other suggestions and comments from the workforce, should be immediately acted upon by changing the checklist or by responding to the trade person regarding the issue they raised. Doing this accomplishes two things. 1) It indicates the high level of support, by management, for the PM program, and 2) it recognizes the importance of the trade person's commitment to the financial well being of the manufacturing enterprise.

5.4.9.5 The completion of a PM check is recorded in the database (CMMS) and ready for an overall analysis to determine the extent of the PM program success or failure. The individual checklist, though, still has a value to the program. A die-specific evaluation (review) should take place at significant milestones in the life of a die. 500K cycles seems an appropriate place to begin such an exercise.

5.4.9.6 To do this, all of that die's completed checklists come into consideration. They can be kept in loose-leaf binders according to die number. Even though specific details/components of a die can be up/down graded between the cycles according to the direct observations of the attendant trade person, the entire tool must also be scrutinized regarding life expectancy and quality throughput. The periodic review is the time to re-evaluate the maintenance needs of any specific tool. Moving the tool to a higher cycle count PM check will save the costs of maintenance but, it should never decrease reliability and throughput quality. After the review, all checklists prior to that particular 500K review should be stored in a "life of tool" file folder to be kept until the die becomes obsolete or its replacement is being re-designed by the engineering staff.

5.5 Benefits

5.5.1 The following examples occurred at the author's stamping plant and show some benefit from a mature PM program. After the "firefights" are history, more time is available to perfect the entire manufacturing process. What seemed impossible prior to PM became a regular occurrence after sanity returned to the stamping/tooling area of the facility.

Example 1   Mating inner and outer door panels became much easier when press tonnage was prescribed for each panel. This discovery was made possible because tonnage was recorded for each panel-run and an enterprising foreperson from the assembly area decided to research various components that comprised his area of responsibility. Although this was not a result of PM, the plant benefited because the data was recorded along with other production information that did relate to maintenance. Quality assemblies directly resulted from this exercise in "minutia", much like a "gift" for picking up pebbles along the main path.

Example 2   TS16949-20XX requirements for continuous improvement led die design engineers to access the collected data to avoid designing failure into their tooling. Complexity ratings, individual failures and mean time to repair played a part in their final decisions. The eventual outcome will be determined and evaluated based on data that will be collected in the future.

The point is: data provides the basis for improvement. The two example activities would not have been possible without the baseline provided by the collected data.

6. TS16949-20XX compatibility

6.1 Definitions:

6.1.1   To meet the standards of TS16949-20XX, a manufacturing process must be effective, documented, improvable and sustainable. Elements of the PM process include:

Bill of materials: in this text, it is called a blueprint booklet

Blueprint Booklet: Contains a listing of all standard, perishable details with accurate dimensions and enough data to reproduce that detail for replacement.

Checklists: used to specify the regular maintenance activities;

Code: Any term, acronym, phrase or symbol utilized as a form of designation for any recordable event.

Common Codes with location: Makes the records sortable and quantifiable as it provides an indication of a recurrent problem.

Computerized Maintenance Management System: (CMMS): Records every incidence of failure.

Downtime: (DT) Downtime occurs when a press or other manufacturing equipment is idled for any reason. It is no longer producing a salable product.

Downtime documentation: Records those failures that cause production stoppage into a CMMS.

Mean Time Between Failure: (MTBF) tracks reliability by measuring the number of hits between each die failure or stoppage during the production process.

Mean Time To Repair: (MTTR): Provides a discipline to track the severity of a problem. The severity is measured by the amount of time needed to repair the failure.

PM Champion: A Champion will be a shift superintendent or a manager at the plant staff level. This person will have the ability and inclination to set performance goals and standards for the supervisors under their authority. They are responsible for designing meaningful reports and identifying the appropriate metrics by which the PM initiative will be measured.

PM Coordinator: The primary responsibility of the PM Coordinator is to market the program and develop it in a logical method consistent with the plant environment and politics. The coordinator must thoroughly understand the process and be committed to the success of die PM. They must also employ the talents and abilities of a management "Champion" to ascertain and develop the methods necessary to ensure success for all concerned.

Preventive Maintenance: (PM) is a process that provides for regular, scheduled maintenance activities. The activities are determined by a particular operation. In general, it means taking the tooling apart and checking components for wear and tear and, then, re-working those components until they are again able to flawlessly perform their primary function. (For purposes of this book, "primary function" means drawing, flanging, forming, lifting, punching, piercing, striking and trimming.)

Recurrent Problems: Easily identified when common codes with a location indicator are used. This is the primary value of a PM program that is supported with an appropriate CMMS.

Recordable Incident (RI) Recordable Incident is a term to describe any occurrence that stops the manufacturing equipment from producing a salable product. Recordable incidents range from a dimpled panel or a missing punch hole to an end-of-run changeover. Legitimate stoppages are recorded as well as those caused by failures of the process itself.

Review Procedure: evaluates the effectiveness of any part – or all parts – of the PM program. The review will include all incidents of failure, by code, and issues discovered during normally scheduled PM activities.

Supervisory Oversight: Interaction between the trade person and the shop facilities that enables the process as well as the remedial actions that might become necessary to correct any failure of the tooling.

When to start/stop a procedure: A comprehensive review procedure will identify and remove any activity that is unnecessary to the PM checklist.

6.2 Checklists

6.2.1 Generic, operation-specific checklists are located in the appendix. However, each facility (usually) has its own approach to die maintenance. Understanding that the ultimate goal is to have a customized checklist for each and every tool, the starting point for each tool are generic lists for each type of die being used to make parts. This "generic" list will be used for the initial start-up period and then altered, as the specific tool requires. Ask for help from trades. They work with the tooling on a day-to-day basis and can identify every maintenance need that they have addressed during the tenure of their service in the plant.

6.2.2 Customize the checklist at 200K hits. That is, review the first few checklists, read the comments made by the person completing the checklist/work order, and alter the generic list until it reflects the specific needs of a specific tool and "save as" the "custom" list with its own tag. This new and specific checklist can then be updated after each PM check, if need be.

6.2.3 The checklist can be designed in a spreadsheet, or preventive maintenance, software package. It should be an easy procedure to make changes. Or to add features. It might be good to know how long it took to complete the Preventive Maintenance check, for example. It helps to know if it was returned to the press in operating condition. Did it achieve first-panel capability?

6.2.4   The comments section, which should be included on the actual checklist, can be used to identify circumstances present on the tool that may be a sign of another trade's problem.

6.3. Bill of Material

6.3.1   A sample blueprint booklet is included in the appendix. One should be prepared for each die in the plant. Since the blueprints are designed to be used, they should be kept in a file or binder near where the corresponding dies are maintained. A master copy should be kept in a master file by the PM coordinator. Each copy is a "Controlled Document" and its cover must provide the information concerning aging, supervisory oversight, etc.

6.3.2   Purchased details and their official manufacturer's ordering codes should be listed by location on the die. Altered sizes of wear plates must be recorded so that replacements can be made directly from the data recorded in the blueprint booklet. The booklet is also a good place to record die-specific data (weight, f-b, r-l, blank size/ material, etc.) along with the number of slides and a detailed account of pertinent information relative to the slides. Every piece and every detail becomes an entry in the booklet. Every engineering change must be recorded as well.

6.3.3   This blueprint booklet will become the most important and most used document in the maintenance area.

6.3.4   A good addition to the booklet is a Hole Chart. Simply put, the hole chart is a graphic or drawing of any particular part with all holes numbered and called out. Each call-out contains the exact size of the desired hole, the manufacturer's code for the punch and button used to pierce the hole, and the exact use for which the hole will be used. It is useful anytime the production process stops because of a broken punch or button as it quickly identifies the culprit and supplies the necessary data that is needed to order the appropriate replacement from the crib or vending machine.

6.4 Review procedure

6.4.1   There comes a time in the life of a tool when its life must be reviewed and its misdeeds evaluated. That time should come at 250,000 hits (varies according to the design and composition of the particular tool). A review procedure should include an evaluation of each of the five PM checklists, performance data relative to die-related downtime (DT) charged to the tooling, and, of course, the actual condition of the tool at the time of its review.

6.4.2   The purpose of the review is to make a decision relative to any change in the cycle-based PM process for that die. For example: zero incidents of DT might move the tool to a longer cycle (from 50K cycles to 100K cycles); one or two incidents may mean that the tool is maintained at its present cycle; while three or more DT incidents could move the die to a lower cycle count PM schedule. This part of the evaluation process must be coupled with a review of the PM checklists (which hold comments about general die condition and parts replaced).

6.4.3   It is a "toss-up" decision whether to include the occasional broken punch as a DT incident. After all, most punches are relatively cheap, easily broken and easily replaced.

6.4.4   After the appropriate decision is made, the finding should be entered onto the evaluation document and all checklists, repair records and DT reports should be stapled together, placed in a physical file and kept until the next iteration of that tooling is designed. Continuous improvement practices should require that performance history is considered before the re-design of a particular set of tooling is accomplished. Such carefully preserved documentation will help avoid the problem of designing failure into new tooling

6.5 Computerized Maintenance Management System (CMMS)

6.5.1   Purchase of a software system should be approached with caution. While it is not absolutely necessary to possess a CMMS to operate an effective die PM process, the amount of data collected and analyzed almost requires that one is available for use. There are suitable CMMS software programs available on the open market. Some are readily customizable and some are not. The primary caution is that most available software is oriented toward machine and equipment maintenance.

6.5.2   In that milieu, completed tasks are the main consideration and, therefore, the primary evaluation of effectiveness is the number of tasks completed in a day, week, month, etc. When it comes to sheet metal stamping, the primary metric is the cost avoidance dollar associated with tooling-related downtime. The difference is that identical machinery is manufactured for many applications and empirical data is plentiful. A 100HP electric motor will operate the same as every other 100HP motor. That means that certain "tasks" can be prescribed with the confidence that, if completed, the motor will continue to operate efficiently.

6.5.3   Tooling is not so easily compared. Each die is pretty much unique in that each die performs an operation on a particular sheet metal part. Data can only be collected beginning when the die is placed in service and comparisons can be made only after performance data is collected for a period of time. That is the reason that every bit of data is collected and stored, preferably on some sort of CMMS.

6.5.4   Larger companies, especially those with remote design and engineering centers, might find some benefit with a mainframe application. Even so, a logical approach is to purchase single user "off the shelf" maintenance software. Developing the PM program on a simple application will allow the user to identify shortcomings, as well as possible enhancements, to the final software product.

6.5.5   TS16949-20XX requires basic record keeping, analysis and continuous improvement. On the way to fulfilling those requirements, a mainframe CMMS can also provide the manufacturer with an abundance of ancillary benefits as well. A population of terminals on the plant floor will facilitate the entry of maintenance data without the need for a dedicated clerk. Production management data can be accessed seamlessly and allow the DT data to be entered at the source (while allowing the production supervisor to find out whether or not the requested changes/maintenance activities were completed). Direct access to maintenance data will help the designers as they work on the next iteration of tooling.

6.5.6   Whether PC based or mainframe resident, ensure that the software manufacturer will provide continuing service for their product until the software fully supports the PM program.

6.5.7   An important aspect of the maintenance software is that it is the face shown to the world. User-friendly software is an extremely important consideration if the general workforce will access the program. Most households enjoy the use of a personal computer and its resident software. A similar look and feel between the workplace computer and the one at home will serve to enhance understanding and use of the PM software.

6.5.8   Left to their own devices, software engineers and information services (I/S) people will impose onerous security on the new system and, virtually, make it unusable. There is a need for some security. There is, usually, no need for multiple passwords that change on a bi-weekly basis for users that are denied access to information that some I/S person feels is not critical to their area of responsibility. As long as users are specifically identified, their ability to view (only) any information relative to their tool should not be restricted. Data entry should be freely allowed. Changes, however, should be reserved to PM Coordinators (or similar) with an attendant explanation for the requested change.

6.5.9   TS16949-20XX does not require a specific security system. It does require a documented system with management oversight and control. A simple system is best. Simple means that it is easily understood, protected from unauthorized changes, and readily available to those who may need to access the information it contains.

6.6   Downtime

6.6.1   Documentation is an essential element of TS16949-20XX certification. Since the primary metric by which tooling PM will be measured is die-related downtime, then it is essential that all incidents of die-related downtime (D/T) be recorded. The benefit to be realized in this process is that, since it is necessary to develop a means to record die-related D/T, every type of D/T can be easily recorded and eventually analyzed.

6.6.2   The most efficient way to record D/T is through the use of codes. (A sample list of codes is included in the appendix.) Codes allow for the quick sorting of data. By attaching times and duration of specific D/T incidents to specific tools or equipment, the building of a substantial history connected to a tool or machine can be accomplished in relatively short order. The condition of tooling directly affects the operation of the presses that contain it during a production run. Also, the condition of the press directly affects the condition of the tooling. The only way to have a comprehensive tooling PM program is to initiate and operate a concurrent PM program for the presses that hold the tooling.

6.6.3   As previously stated, the intent should be to record everything. Every detail of a stamping process failure is important to someone. If a broad data collection process is in operation and supported by management, there is little difficulty to collect data, by code, which details the cause and affect of any production stoppage. Sure as tomorrow, when the major problems have disappeared (and they will), some engineer will be asked to study some minor cause of D/T. Having heretofore "unimportant" data available for analysis will greatly facilitate that discovery process.

6.6.4   When D/T is recorded, it is not a major concern whether the time is recorded by the minute or by some fraction of an hour. If the production control software uses one method, there is no reason to remake the system. There is one important step to take. That step is to assign a value to the time. This is a job for the comptroller who has access to the necessary records to identify the value of the equipment and the floor space occupied by the stamping presses. Single, small OBI presses might only be valued at one or two hundred dollars an hour. An A++ transfer press might be valued at $1500 an hour. Whatever the amount, it should be used to place a dollar value on the D/T associated with a press or a piece of tooling.

6.6.5   To facilitate data collection, information should be gathered by those who normally record production control information. The two most important considerations are the preservation and integrity of the data. This data will be part of the review procedure and the recorder must be responsible enough to assign the right code to a problem and, in turn, they must be afforded some "protection" from the mechanizations of a supervisor who might be unwilling to explain the existence of failure within their process.

6.6.6   The evaluation process should include a joining of D/T failure codes with repair codes so that an investigation can identify the proper solution to subsequent, similar failures. Coupling D/T codes with repair codes will help to ensure the reporting accuracy required by the QS standard.

6.7   Mean Time to Repair

6.7.1   (MTTR) can be one of the metrics associated with the tooling maintenance program. It is internationally recognized as such and, therefore, an acceptable standard of measure for TS16949-20XX. At the outset, MTTR will be significant. Uncared for tooling deteriorates rapidly as one problem affects another and each failure exacerbates another.

6.7.2   As the tooling comes under control and the PM program matures, MTTR will decline as the problems become isolated and easier to deal with. Since this measure is a program metric, effectiveness will be shown as a comparison to pre-preventive maintenance. That means that care should be taken early on in the PM program deployment to capture the existing MTTR data. Management has a right to expect an increase in performance for the financial and moral support they have provided. The information they receive should be presented in a language they understand. MTTR is their language.

6.7.3   Providing this same data to the advanced engineering department will assist them as they design the next iteration of existing tools. MTTR data can be an indicator of a design problem. A problem that may be easily remedied at the design stage since all components necessary to address a fix will be present. MTTR will provide a cost evaluation of the problems inherent in the designed tooling. The cost to repair – over the life of the tool – is justification to spend a little time to redesign the tooling to eliminate major, and minor, failures.

6.7.4   Another benefit to adding MTTR to the plant PM toolbox is to improve repair techniques. Making quick repairs to tool steel sections, for example, can lead to more problems due to improper pre and post-heat operations that accelerate steel degeneration. Comparing the quick repair to a properly prepared steel being pre-heated, welded with an appropriate rod, and post-heated according to accepted standards can be accomplished through MTTR in combination with mean time between failures (MTBF). The currency provided by MTTR can lead to, among other things, a weld process improvement program that will improve the MTBF numbers.

6.8   Mean Time Between Failures

6.8.1   MTBF At the outset of a new PM program, MTBF should be modified to MTBSF (mean time between specific failures). With tools that are not under control, failures can be almost constant and MTBF numbers will not be meaningful. The only measure can be MTBSF so that confidence can build in a new system that will eventually ensure full-run capability.

6.8.2   To measure MTBSF, a "failure" code is needed. A location code should be added as well. It should not be left to memory to determine whether a problem with one broken punch is an isolated incident; is a part of many broken punches (which can indicate the need for a new supplier of punches); or is it one punch location that breaks many times (which can indicate a design problem). In addition, burrs, form deterioration, galled wear plates may quickly identify a problem with press deterioration.

6.8.3   The main point is that MTBSF, augmented with a location code, should be part of the evaluation process so that an accurate picture can be composed of the effectiveness of the new, comprehensive die PM program. TS16949-20XX considers this an oversight and evaluation procedure to ensure that neither time nor capital is wasted with unnecessary activity.

6.9 When to start/stop

6.9.1   Under TS16949-20XX, if a process is in place, the expectation is that everything in the facility is a part of that process. With that in mind, the time to launch the process is immediately after the process has been defined and the documentation is determined. From a practical point of view, considering that the tooling is deteriorating every day, it makes sense to quickly include every tool in the die PM program. The only valid reason for not doing so is physical limitation. Without question, documenting performance can begin immediately and will serve to help evaluate process performance as the PM program develops across the entire spectrum of working tools.

6.10 Current tools

6.10.1   While the goal is to compile a "biography" of each and every tool, the current tools will, of necessity, have their story told as of day one of program launch. These tools will never fully recover from neglect. The goal for them is to stabilize their condition and strive for trouble-free production runs.

6.10.2   During regular visits to the die maintenance area, each die should be considered to be in the rehabilitation mode. The guidance system is the primary candidate. Worn heel/wear plates can be replaced. So can brass bushings for guide pins. Obviously, care is taken to accommodate the effect that these changes will have on working elements of the die. Each visit to the die maintenance area can mean one more improvement and, as these improvements accumulate, the performance of even the worst die should show some measure of improvement. Remember, that "measure" is based on the accumulated performance data of that particular tooling.

6.11 Blueprint Books

6.11.1   As each tool is rehabbed, the blueprint book for each die can be updated – or filled in – to reflect the actual conditions that are present in each die. This book is an important document – a controlled document for TS16949-20XX purposes – but program launch should not wait for its completion. The book should, though, be completed by the first review at 250,000 (or 5th PM). New tools should arrive at the stamping plant with all the pertinent data completed by the build source.

6.11.2 As conditions change within each tool, the blueprint book must be updated and the previous book discarded or, at least, marked as out-dated. During the launch activity (for a new product line, not the PM program launch), especially, there will be some number of engineering changes made to implement new fit and form needs. Care must be taken to record these changes in the blueprint booklet so that these changes can be considered during normal PM activity.

6.12 Reviews

6.12.1 Cycle-based reviews should be initiated immediately whenever a die is entered into the PM program. This means that cycle counts must begin immediately and, after the prescribed number of cycles, a review will take place. The tendency is to wait for some milestone to be achieved before the cycles start counting. There should be no "waiting".

6.12.2 One exception is the wait to launch a set of tools into the PM program based on a capability chart that schedules the PM checklist activities according to available time for completion. For example: suppose that there are numerous series of five dies that produce parts for the same automobile, refrigerator, etc; two people are all that are available to perform the PM checks; one shift is what is required to complete each check; then, a single shift work schedule will allow that only one set of five dies can be checked in a standard week. Anticipating 5000 units per week production rate, the first set of dies will be ready for their first PM check in ten weeks after the cycle count begins. To keep the discipline of cycle counts intact, then the second set of five dies will not begin the cycle counting until one week later than the first set of five dies.

6.12.3 Scheduling dies for PM can be a complicated process. It is best to work up a spreadsheet and enter dates that reflect certain expectations relative to production counts. This exercise will quickly indicate the scope of PM activity and, probably, give a pretty good idea how many die makers will be needed to successfully implement the PM program.

6.12.4 The benefits of collecting data and performing systematic checks on any particular tool is especially manifest when performance data can be provided to the design engineers who are planning the next iteration of a particular tool. The design source, armed with actual data, can be expected to eliminate recurring failures and facilitate increased productivity by fine tuning the design of the tool. TS16949-20XX expect the production/repair source to provide this data and assist in the continuous improvement of working tools.

6.12.5 When dies are de-commissioned, the gathering of data can cease. However, the data must be stored and made available for future study. An "improved" die design must be measured against a previous life to determine whether the design "fix" was successful or not. Therefore, the maintenance software should include a module that allows any data to be archived – stored but available with a small effort. To facilitate the transfer of such information, it should be kept on electronic media in a special database, preferably the company network or intra-net. A hard copy file should also be kept for an ample length of time

6.13 Recurrent problems

6.13.1 The identification of recurring failures is a major benefit of adherence to any quality-oriented manufacturing discipline. In all cases, data will provide the road map to detect the causes of failure. Complete data, that is. There is little use to collect some data some of the time. If the data collecting exercise is functioning, every bit of data should be collected and available for analysis.

6.13.2 One broken punch tells a small story. Maybe it's an anomaly, maybe not. Many broken punches could be caused by a press malfunction. Or they might indicate the need to find a new supplier of pierce punches. One punch broken many times is, most likely, a design defect and could warrant an extensive redesign of the tool. Burrs and form deterioration might indicate improper weld procedures and heat-treating; or a problem with the sheet metal being used to produce the part.

6.13.3 Excessively worn wear plates are indicators of poor die design or, more likely, press failures. The list can go on and on and on. The main point is that analysis depends on properly collected and preserved data. TS16949-20XX expect that the manufacturer's process will include the collection of data and its provision to appropriate end-users.

6.13.4 Since the resolution process relies on accumulated data; TS16949-20XX demands a written or documented process. Terms must be defined. Processes must be described. After all, a design engineer doesn't appreciate complaints about a tool design that are based on a haphazard and arbitrary analysis of sketchy data by a less than credentialed individual. However, a clearly written and exactly followed process for identifying recurring failures provides that same engineer with the opportunity to improve future designs for their production "customers"

6.13.5 By reporting general die performance data to advanced manufacturing, PM can be responsible for dramatic improvements to the overall production operation as it aids the plant to actually achieve real process control. The proper foundation for a credible process evaluation is an abundance of usable, accurate data. The key word is usable. Long-hand text is not usable for general evaluation purposes. It is valuable when researching a specific problem with a specific tool – root cause analysis-wise. But, process evaluation requires a better tool. A code.

6.14 Common Codes

6.14.1 A code is a simple device that allows a database to sort through the volumes of stored information and present the compilation in a concise and understandable manner. While that goal is fairly straightforward, the approach one takes is critical to the overall effectiveness and utility of the gathered information.

6.14.2 For example, there can be several ways to describe what caused a burred hole. Bad punch, chipped punch, broken punch, broken button and chipped hole come to mind. There are many other ways to describe this problem and that, itself, becomes a problem. Long-hand entries will sort on the first letter of the entry. This sort requires one to physically review each entry to identify the actual number of similar problems. Why not preempt that slow and laborious activity by agreeing to a specific code to describe the failure? The following lists illustrate a complete system of codes that can identify every class of failures that stop a press from producing parts. Only a few deal with die-related issues. However, in keeping with the intent to gather every bit of data possible, every instance of press stoppage must be recorded and made available to each department so that a proper resolution can be made to the entire manufacturing process.

See "Downtime Codes Example" in Appendix

6.14.3 The three-letter code is determined by each department to reflect their specific needs. Industry-wide, each set of codes will be very similar from plant to plant, company to company. However, maintaining a common code for an entire industry would be unmanageable and unnecessary.

6.14.4 The importance of this set of codes cannot be stressed enough. Also, the codes should reflect the specific processes within a particular plant. Preferably, a maintenance crew from each department should meet and determine the proper codes for their own use. Production's responsibility, then, becomes the accurate recording of each failure and the actual minutes (or hours) of DT associated with a particular failure.

6.14.5 All equipment Every piece of operating equipment must be considered and each component of the stamping process must be included when codes are established. In short, every minute of plant operation is accounted for when the day is done. Including lunch break, rest periods and any idle time will ensure the integrity of the data collection process. The collected data becomes the basis for evaluating the entire plant maintenance program. It must be above reproach.

6.15 Repair Codes

6.15.1 Once the data begins to collect, repairs to the culprit tools can be accomplished and related to the recorded failure. When this happens, it will become evident that a further description must be applied to the failure. For example, a DBU (punch/button failure) could be caused by a chipped punch, broken dowel/loose retainer, impaired slug shed, or any number of things. The goal is to identify the actual cause of the failure and attach that cause to the D/T failure code. This activity will close the loop and allow a very accurate analysis of the failure by interested parties.

6.15.2 Again, the most effective codes are determined by those who do the work. The actual code should be four parts and include: primary function (trim, pierce, form, etc.); effect of the failure on the part produced (burr, dent, etc.); specific component causing the failure (punch, button, riser, spring, etc.); and location of the failure (X, Y & Z axis). Obviously, this code provides a more detailed explanation of the failure's cause. It is much more specific and each trade should strive to include a code for any possible failure that can occur to their equipment/tooling.

6.15.3 The pressroom supervisor is responsible for the accurate application of Downtime Codes to account for every minute of available press time. The skilled tradesperson is responsible for identifying and recording the actual repair code that describes the real cause of the failure. The PM Coordinator is responsible for recording both codes and the times associated with them. It then falls to the supervisory level person to periodically review the data, review the panels produced and make adjustments to the maintenance process regarding any particular set of tools. This inherent review program requires that the repair codes be quite detailed in their description of any particular failure. As tooling is changed, repair codes might need to be added to properly reflect newly possible causes of failure

6.16 Part Replacement:

6.16.1 Significant good can be achieved by adding a part replacement module to the CMMS. It can help determine the functionality and quality of any purchased parts. It will help to identify recurring problems resulting from design deficiencies – in the absence of a location code module in the CMMS. It will also verify "float" quantities held by the tool crib as well as usage statistics and cross-reference checks of actual throughput in the cribbing area.

6.17 Mean Time To Repair:

6.17.1 (MTTR) is a popular method by which to measure program effectiveness. Since it is a metric that indicates how quickly a corrective action can be taken and a tool is put back in service, it has a limited value in a PM program evaluation. Obviously, the more frequent the failure, the more experience one has in making a repair, the shorter the MTTR becomes. The PM program should focus on reducing the number of failures and on avoiding future problems by making a permanent fix to the tool. However, most every CMMS, off the shelf, will include a module that computes MTTR for the manager level employee.

6.18 Oversight

6.18.1 Primary responsibility for process compliance, as previously stated, falls on the shoulders of the supervisory level employee. The PM Coordinator and the PM Champion, who manage the PM program, should respond to the concerns of the supervisor as they relate to the periodic review, which is conducted at specific intervals in the production cycle. To provide data for this review, the supervisors can assist the PM program by using a formal, standard shift line-up form that provides basic information about the tools being repaired or undergoing a PM check. The tool number, hours worked, and a description of the work being done (so it can be assigned a proper repair code) are necessary components of this "line-up" document. This information can then be entered into the CMMS accurately and in a timely manner.

6.18.2 TS16949-20XX require a control on documents. Using a specific form for line-ups satisfies this need. Retention of the daily line-up depends on whether the plant management feels the need to micro-manage the maintenance process. Usually, it is not necessary to retain the line-up after the information has been transferred to the CMMS. Ownership of the line-up process may remain with the supervisor as long as the PM Coordinator has rights of final review concerning the design of the form.

7. Preventive Maintenance Integration

7.1 Definition:

Using and improving the maintenance process for every element that affects the manufacturing process.

Checklists: Used to specify the regular maintenance activities;

Die Storage   (DS) Die Storage is that floor space which is dedicated to the storage of production tooling in close proximity to its respective maintenance area.

Downtime   (DT) Downtime occurs when a press or other manufacturing equipment is idled for any reason. It is no longer producing a salable product.

Dock Audit   The last quality-check of stamped parts before they are shipped to the customer.

First Time Capability (FTC) First Time Capability is the ability of a manufacturing process to produce a salable product from the initial (first) cycle of the manufacturing equipment. That is, without any further adjustment.

Just-In-Time   (JIT) Just-In-Time production is a system that produces only enough salable product to maintain the "fill" of an assembly process for one day's production.

Last Panel Analysis (LPA) Last Panel Analysis is the inspection of the last panel produced in the stamping process. This inspection should direct the course of activity during the period of time before that tooling is placed in service the next time. (i.e.: storage; steam cleaning; sharpening; repair)

Preventive Maintenance (PM) Preventive Maintenance is a process that provides for regular, scheduled maintenance activities. The particular activities are determined by a particular operation. In general, it means taking the tooling apart and checking components for wear and tear and, then, re-working those components until they are again able to flawlessly perform their primary function. (For purposes of this book, "primary function" means drawing, flanging, forming, lifting, punching, piercing, striking and trimming.)

PM Coordinator The primary responsibility of the PM Coordinator is to market the program and develop it in a logical method consistent with the plant environment and politics. The coordinator must thoroughly understand the process and be committed to the success of die PM. They must also employ the talents and abilities of a management "Champion" to ascertain and develop the methods necessary to ensure success for all concerned.

Run-to-Run The time from when the last panel of a production run is placed in an appropriate rack for conveyance to the shipping dock or customer to the point when the first panel of the next (different) production run in that press or press line is picked up for placement in an appropriate rack.

Panel Storage (PS) Panel Storage refers to the plant floor space that is occupied by salable product prior to its shipment to its purchasing entity.

Total Productive Maintenance TPM is a process that seeks to eliminate unnecessary maintenance activities while using procedures that deliver just-in-time capabilities through use of a trained, involved and empowered work force assisted by the robust control of available equipment. Not easy to achieve. Impossible to achieve without a decent PM program and will be considerably easier with a robust PdM technology.

PM Champion A Champion will be a shift superintendent or a manager at the plant staff level. A person with the ability and inclination

155

to set performance goals and standards for the supervisors under their authority. They are responsible for designing meaningful reports and identifying the appropriate metrics by which the PM initiative will be measured.

PM Committee   The PM Committee is charged with guiding, and then maintaining, the PM implementation process from the plant floor. They will meet to add or subtract from the existing list of DT codes and repair codes. This committee will help gain support for the program among their fellow workers. If the members represent a variety of disciplines, there will soon be interactions between their respective departments which will use the data and procedures to further their own ends.

Tool Machine PM   The tooling PM program is designed to improve the tooling maintenance function, it only stands to reason that expediting the process is desirable as well. The most productive step that can be taken is to form tool-machine centers that truly serve the needs of the trade people who maintain the tooling. Just the exercise of investigating machine tools will be beneficial. New technology will have a significant impact on maintenance and machining functions. Computer driven, 5-axis machining centers can be used in a variety of money-saving ways to enhance operations. Die separators and portable Diffracto™ machines can also improve the maintenance function. Of course, the simple drill, saw, surface grinder and Bridgeport-type machine need to be in ample supply.

Press PM   Thermal, sonic, and oil-related (tribology) technologies serve to identify possible and impending failures to stamping presses and drive motors. A tooling PM program will never fully realize its potential unless there is a comparable PM process for the presses that activate their potential.

Assembly PM All the robots, stations, welders, printers and associated electronics are included in an Assembly PM program. Regular checks are necessary and timing is dependent on total count of panels processed/finished by the operation.

Automation PM   Transfer bars, pick-up fingers, transfer trucks and bucks, associated electronic devices, panel lubrication and blank feeders are all covered by an automation centered PM program.

Reliability Centered Maintenance (RCM): According   to maintenanceresources.com, RCM is a process used to determine what must be done to ensure that any physical asset continues to do whatever its users want it to do in its present operating context. In other words: how little maintenance can be done before tooling or equipment fails to perform as expected.

7.2   Process Improvement

7.2.1   Without question, the most fundamental value of a fully developed, comprehensive PM program is that, carried to its logical extension, every process that touches the tooling process must improve to allow the tooling maintenance program to fully benefit the entire stamping enterprise. Areas such as facilities, production, material handling, die setting, press maintenance, automation, etc all touch the tooling process. It will be impossible to optimize the function of tooling if, say, presses continue to malfunction and cause damage to the tooling. Conveyors that add debris to a panel, cause by shredded belting, will easily cause more coining and burrs. Transfer bars that malfunction will continue to damage surfaces as they destroy themselves. Coolants, lubrication and the equipment that deliver them to the stamping process must be adequately maintained to achieve optimum performance objectives.

7.2.2   Call it continuous improvement, call it what you will, it must happen. And, it's possible. Remember, the means to identify any problem contained in the stamping process is available (if the previously mentioned system of downtime codes is used). Tackling each problem one by one means that the changes will occur incrementally and can be more easily handled. Time is money and the sooner PM is implemented the quicker savings will occur. However, the goal is a long term one and patience and persistence are the key elements that will guarantee success.

7.3 Cutting Solutions

7.3.1   Today's technology pertaining to cutting solutions is the coin of the phrase "cutting edge". That means that it is very much experimental. To provide the best product, it must be constantly adjusted to keep up with the ever-changing assemblage of cutters, materials, coatings, etc. Hence, the laundry list of part/product numbers one sees when perusing such a catalogue of "solutions" to the machinist's cutting needs. These companies, through their representatives, willingly "partner" with manufacturers of every stripe to find the right product to do any and every particular job. To use that resource to maximum benefit, the plant must know what is being used, what it is used to cut, and how well it performs based on an experienced machinist's personal knowledge – and then recorded for access at the appropriate time. This may seem, to a plant manager, a very small consideration. The issue is large in importance to the trade person who uses the cutting oils on a daily basis. Who might know more about the cutting process? Manager? Machinist?

7.3.2   Cutting oils and coolants are almost synonymous in shop parlance. "Almost" being the operative word. As opposed to cutting fluid, coolants are deemed to be reusable and are constantly recycled through the pump and back to the tool bit. Commonly, the coolant is a consumable and the belief is that simply refilling the tank will maintain the system. Not so. Bacteria and particulates can, over a short time, contaminate the solutions and destroy any benefits associated with using these chemicals. And they will smell too. Regular, thorough cleanings and coolant replacement will ensure proper operation and reception of the full benefit of a costly component of the machining operation within the entire plant operation.

7.4 Machining

7.4.1   Since most repairs will involve some aspect of machining, it is important that this equipment is in suitable operating condition. Re-cutting a trim edge straight and true will eliminate hand finishing and will also ensure a perpendicular cutting edge that will perform for an extended period without failure. Even bench tool grinders for sharpening drill bits should be properly maintained and have a PM checklist to be used when performing routine maintenance. Obviously, drills should drill straight and perpendicular holes; diemakers' friends should grind a surface square with the bottom; saws must do their job quickly and effectively. This close attention to every piece of equipment may seem like overkill, but properly maintained, these machines will effectively support the repair/maintenance process and reduce the time needed to do so.

7.5 Equipment I.D.

7.5.1   Until the stamping process comes under complete control, repairs to the tooling will remain a primary concern. PM for the machines is a must and to control the control system, a logical system of equipment ID tagging must be developed to ensure positive identification within the computer maintenance management system (CMMS). TS16949-20XX requires a system of periodic calibration. A regular program can be more easily evaluated than a sporadic (*read: none*) system. The primary function of the plant machinery is to provide part duplication. Numerical control or basic part duping will require that the machining function is performed flawlessly. Calibrations ensure perfection.

7.5.2   Documented proof must exist that every piece of equipment is properly maintained on a periodic basis. Using a CMMS will make this aspect of the control system easier to accomplish. In fact, most CMMS's will suggest a logical system to follow. There are some, with simple needs, that will choose not to purchase a full-blown CMMS and will develop their own with existing software. The pitfall to avoid is using current descriptions of the existing equipment.

Samples:	old mill by the door (OMBTD)	or MM1
	New mill in bay one (NMIBO)	or MM2
	Bullard mill (BM)	or RM1
	Shaper 1 (SO)	or SM1
	Vertical mill in die shop (VMIDS)	or SM2

7.5.3   The right way is to develop fields within the database selected that further describe the equipment and which can change when the equipment is moved, altered, sold or scrapped.

7.6   Machine Calibration

7.6.1   The aircraft and aerospace manufacturing industries have little and no problem with machine calibration. They live with it and perform it often. Mostly, they produce consumables – parts that must be exactly machined and that must fit together at final assembly. Other industries may not need that capability. A good machinist, given enough time, can make any part to specification. Or so it has been for many years. Nowadays, just-in-time manufacturing might not always make parts that must fit perfectly together. But that process has another factor to consider: Time. Unless the manufacturer is willing to support a very costly inventory of tooling details that might fail during the stamping process, rapid repair/replacement of a failed component is necessary.

7.6.2   The obvious answer is to purchase the necessary equipment and train machine repair people to calibrate in-house. In a smaller operation, it may be necessary to hire an outside provider to perform the task in an on-going capacity. It may sound expensive, but, improving quality; improving productivity; improving reparability; and improving up-time have values that can more than off-set the expense.

7.7   Variation

7.7.1   When the customer provides math data to support the part being produced in a vendor's plant, modern numerically controlled (NC) equipment will ensure that the machining process does not cause variation to the tooling that makes the part. Sounds easy. However, there is a critical need to PM that equipment as well as explore other opportunities to optimize this important process. Calibration has already been covered. So have coolants and cutter oils. The manufacturer will be able to provide a PM checklist for any product they make. The only things left to work on are variables. And, there should be very few of those to contend with.

7.7.2   The process improvements made to the die setting function (die sandwiches; locators; etc.) will now support set-up optimization for the NC machines. If the point of quick die change is to quickly and accurately locate die shoes on a press bolster for the fast and efficient clamping equipment, why can't that same process now be used to accurately locate die shoes on the tables of NC machines? The same areas that accept toggle clamps and hydraulic clamping devices on the press bolster can be used to hold the die shoes on the table of an NC machine. (Another example of the theory that it is impossible to optimize any process without causing the optimization of every other process that touches it.)

7.8   Repeating the Process

7.8.1   On the journey to attainment of total process control, which a comprehensive PM process enables, it is necessary to bring every part of the process along as the maintenance program develops. And, it's easier to do that incrementally. If the die room is the focus of attention at the outset, the checklist development for each particular piece of machinery located in or adjacent to the die shop will provide the basis and form for similar machinery in other parts of the plant. In other words, it gets easier as the process matures because the process can be simply applied by using the same or similar schedules/checklists throughout.

7.9   Production Control

7.9.1   Production is a process that must be controlled. Oftentimes, that control is manifested by computer software that maintains daily counts, various levels of throughput, scrap counts, and (hopefully) downtime that results from any type of failure. All this is important and necessary. What is also needed is awareness by management that the production process must accommodate the need to maintain the tooling. The production manager is prone to use every minute of every day to stamp parts because "it's what we do". They allow very little maintenance time but find themselves facing an increasing amount of repair time. Incredibly, repair time becomes acceptable because it finally becomes unavoidable and, ultimately, the production manager is only held accountable for throughput with an allowance for tooling or equipment failure that is "beyond their control".

7.9.2   In reality, this manager, this department IS responsible if they force tooling failure by a refusal to grant sufficient time to properly maintain the plant equipment and tooling that is the mainstay of the company's profit picture.

7.10 Quality

7.10.1 First and foremost, quality is the responsibility of every department, every shift, every work crew, and every individual in a sheet metal stamping facility. The advent of transfer presses and robotic transfer systems between tandem press operations has taken away a very important quality inspector from the current stamping environment. In particular, that inspector is the production worker who has been displaced in this modern culture. Instead of a press-to-press panel review, the quality inspection is conducted at the delivery end of the operation – and some, fairly new, automatic racking systems are even eliminating that opportunity to inspect the panel before delivery to the assembly operation. All these improvements simply underscore the need to provide a comprehensive die maintenance program that will ensure a measure of quality and reliability to the panels produced by these tools.

7.11 Reliability

7.11.1 Productivity is a good word. Quality is another. When working in concert, the manufacturer is close to achieving optimum performance. That optimum is finally attained when productivity and quality are combined with reliability. Making enough parts, in specification, to meet the assembly schedule of the client guarantees success for most stampers. If that is accomplished without costly downtime or excessive scrap production, then all involved want to repeat that process again and again so as to be competitive with other suppliers in the stamping industry.

7.12 Accuracy

7.12.1 The most strategic role that Process Managers can play in the overall stamping process is to ensure that some semblance of accuracy exists with the downtime reporting system. That means, particularly, that each trade or production-related process member fully participate in the identification of an appropriate coding system for all production-related failures. The completeness and accuracy of these codes will provide the framework for incremental improvements to the entire process. Work crews will be most active identifying problems when they are assured that someone is watching and working to eliminate any costly failures. Correctly identifying a failure will allow for a quicker, more on-target resolution that wastes no time, money, nor physical resources while maintaining or improving the overall quality of the stamped product.

7.13 Quality Assurance Programs

7.13.1 A sure sign that there is little and no process control is the existence of quality assurance programs like dock audits, last panel analysis, first panel capability. Of course, they exist and are, currently, necessary, but the plant's goal should be to get rid of them. They are a waste of time and manpower. Control of the presses, tooling and sheet metal is the main concern and that control is accomplished with appropriate maintenance programs. Checking panels after they are formed is too late - unless scrap is the desired product of the process. Maximum material throughput is achieved when downtime is restricted to the six or eight minutes required to change the dies and transfer system.

7.14 Automation et al

7.14.1 Obviously. The tooling that this book is most concerned with is the stamping die. However, other classes of tooling directly affect this essential element of the stamping process. Automation and other part transfer equipment can adversely affect the performance of the dies they serve. The fingers, bucks, clamps, etc. may be attached to equipment like transfer bars, shuttles, idle stations, etc. but that which directly contacts the part itself is considered tooling. Too often, little attention is paid to these incidentals, which can greatly assist or damage the part transfer phase of a modern transfer press stamping operation.

7.14.2 A good starting point to develop a complimentary tooling PM program is to start at the head of the production press line and write down every piece of equipment that is involved with the process. Next, with the respective trade people, develop comprehensive PM checklists for every element that was identified during the walk-through and then, prove the checklists and cycle frequencies under actual run conditions. Add and subtract according to actual experience. Replicate the program for every production line. Since each line will contain similar equipment, development time will be close to nil. Obviously, that will mean that PM leadership will be necessary for the additional departments who have ownership of all the ancillary equipment involved in the stamping process.

7.14.3 Incredibly, welded, homemade fingers that require constant adjustment from die-set to die-set are deemed cheaper than the more expensive, manufactured transfer clamps and fingers that require a single adjustment during the life of the particular product model. Apparently, the only time a trade person's time (constantly fiddling with homemade concoctions of "tooling") is considered costly is when they ask for a raise. To support the productivity of a million dollar press, it seems academic to have a set of pre-set fingers and clamps for each and every part produced by that particular press. Not only does such a set of fingers and clamps reduce variation in the process, but they also allow the opportunity to obtain world-class die change times and eliminate costly downtime. They also reduce the chance that a finger or clamp will fail and cause damage to the all-important stamping die.

7.15 Facilities

7.15.1 While facilities do not directly affect the stamping die, the delivery of water and adequate electricity directly impact the performance of the equipment that operates or alters that tooling. Although chemicals are added for enhancement purposes, water is the essential element used when a milling machine alters a die for an approved engineering change or when an essential repair is required to restore the tool to original condition.

7.15.2 Electricity powers almost everything in the plant. It is almost a requirement that modern technology, such as an infrared camera, is used to detect "hot-spots" caused by faulty electrical equipment. Too much electricity is a problem. Too little electricity can be a bigger problem. The small amount needed to energize proximity switches and die protection devices must be delivered so that essential activities, such as these devices perform, can be relied on to prevent failure. A companion equipment PM program will provide solid support for the comprehensive tooling PM program under current discussion.

7.16 Floor Space Allocation

7.16.1 There are two aspects of floor space allocation: space to maintain the tooling; and panel storage. Maintenance space should be designed to meet the needs of tool and die makers, their tools, machine tools, etc. and it must address the requirements of die storage, die transportation, washing, intra-plant traffic, welding, all the while adapting and adopting new technologies as they become available.

7.16.2 As the tooling PM program matures, the need to store finished panels as "back-up" to the stamping operation will greatly diminish until, after full PM implementation and maturation, a Just-In-Time (JIT) production posture will be possible. PM enables JIT. JIT enables proper service and appropriate cost savings to the end-user or customer. The manufacturer possesses the means to remain or regain profitability through productivity.

7.16.3 While the need to store panels is reduced, the corresponding amount of floor space becomes available for productive use. New profit centers are possible. Jobs are created – a definite plus for the current employees' job security. And, wasteful downtime is greatly reduced because reliable, quality productivity is increased.

7.16.4 A properly maintained die will reliably draw and form panels as it allows their quick and efficient removal to the next station or parts bin. The enhanced performance will reduce the amount of sprayed compounds required to make parts. Obviously, less spray reduces the amount of particulates in the air breathed by plant employees as well as the purity of the air ingested by the running equipment in close proximity to the forming die that helps to foul the air. Filters are costly. Forming compounds are even more costly. PM seems cheap in comparison.

7.17 Tooling Storage

7.17.1 Better use of floor space currently used for panel storage has already been discussed. Controlled storage space for proper protection of the tooling is also an issue. A central area with adequate access and room to maneuver is ideal. Numbered berths in a logical pattern will help to eliminate time lost due to locating a particular die or set of dies.

7.17.2 Simple tags can provide crucial information pertaining to the current location of the tooling. One tag for machine, one for die repair, and another for "in production" should suffice. But the individual conditions of the stamping facility will dictate the proper use and designation of a tagging system. The point here is that storage and location control will be helpful to the die set operation and further enhance the possibility of the plant to achieve world-class die change times. This will support proper die maintenance and PM because it helps to optimize an operation that, obviously, impacts the way a die is handled as it is delivered to the stamping press or as it is returned to the die maintenance area for servicing.

7.18 Basic Services

7.18.1 The die is operated by the stamping press; is within the confines of the entire plant. Therefore, a proper PM program that is centered on facilities, or plant equipment, is essential to the full implementation and optimization of a comprehensive tooling PM program. Regular, time-based checks of essential services will ensure that an adequate supply of water, air and electricity are delivered to the stamping operation. The need for equipment maintenance is widely recognized. There are countless books that deal with all the controls and systems needed for a successful Maintenance PM program. This PM program will allow the stamping process to maintain an adequate productive output to provide for a profitable enterprise. Owners like profitability.

7.19 Material Handling

7.19.1 Cranes and the indispensable hilo are vital elements of the material handling operation. However, one must not ignore skids, boxes and part bins. The equipment carries the material and must properly operate to support the manufacturing process. But, the containers can, much too easily, become trash receptacles for any passer-by who is too lazy to find the round cans that have been placed conveniently around the factory. What to do? Train and discipline employees and inspect the container before they are used to hold any part that is shipped to the customer.

7.19.2 OSHA will require regular inspection of plant equipment such as cranes. Their potential for massive damage is well known and, therefore, there is little and no argument that heavy equipment must be maintained on a regular basis to protect the members of the workforce as well as the physical plant. Steel coils do not run well when they have been dropped and subsequently marred by a malfunctioning crane or hoist.

7.19.3 Maintenance of rolling stock such as a hilo involves the battery, the motor, wheels, forks, brakes and chains. Reputable manufacturers of such equipment should provide a comprehensive PM checklist to guide the maintenance staff as it performs periodic checks of the rolling stock. Since many newer hilos are electric, it behooves one to maintain the charger and its ancillary equipment as well.

7.19.4 It is easy to conceive that driver training could be a component of a hilo maintenance program since accident prevention would save the vehicle some damage and safe driving practices would save injury to a worker. Proper techniques would minimize damage to any tooling that may be transported by lift trucks and hilos.

7.20 Dunnage & Containers

7.20.1 Skids can become carriers of oil and stones and all matter of dirt found on the factory floor or in the storage yard. The fact that blanks are often supplied on such skids means that this offal can be readily delivered to the stamping operation and the dies that belong to it. The main offenders are oak skids. However, even plastic skids, unwashed and abused, will become carriers of enough dirt to become dangerous to the stamping process as it relates to blanks being delivered to the first form die.

7.20.2 Boxes should be inspected and cleaned by the press operator before being filled with parts. Since most small parts carried by boxes are going to become a component of a larger weldment, it makes sense to eliminate anything, such as grit, grime, paper, etc., that would slow down the eventual assembly operation. Because the operator may dislike picking through the refuse in the box to find clean parts, because welding machines work better when they unite pieces that are clean and free of debris, and because there is absolutely no value-added consideration related to using part bins for garbage pails, it seems that a vigorous program of cleaning part containers would pay dividends toward a more efficient work process.

7.20.3 A Just in Time operation requires a proper control system for part bins. Standard size bins can easily be interchanged between parts. Therefore, regular cleaning of the bins and removal of the labels will help to eliminate any mis-direction of finished parts due to confusion that can be caused by multiple labels and bar codes.

7.21 Electronics

7.21.1 Today's technology allows corporate design software (such as AutoCAD, Catia, etc.) to directly download math data to NC machines and replicate details that may have suffered catastrophic failure during the stamping operation. This little innovation will trim days from the recovery process. All that is needed is a competent NC machinist and a regular, aggressive calibration schedule.

7.21.2 The NC machine is one more component that helps to make up an efficient and effective substructure that will support the manufacturing process in the daily battle to improve reliability, quality and a new, improved profitability.

7.22 Press PM

7.22.1 In some manufacturing operations, the more something costs, the less care and attention it should receive. So... that logic dictates that the press gets little and (sometimes) no attention until there is a failure that brings production to a halt. Absolutely no one will admit to espousing that line of logic, but actions speak louder than empty words. As stated in a previous chapter, much of this failed reasoning is a direct result of employing the wrong metrics to evaluate the PM program. Because each component of production is vital to the goal of producing, in quantity, parts that meet the customer's specifications, any failure of any part of the system brings every part of the system to a costly halt.

7.22.2 Obviously, a stamping press is the main component of a stamping operation because it, usually, costs the most. Why, then, do so many stampers have an abundance of presses that stand idle so that a worker can be moved from press to press as one failure after another occurs during the course of the day? It would seem that this approach is a rather costly counterpoint to an effective preventive maintenance program. There is no better example of the mutuality of dependence as between a stamping die and a stamping press. Each un-maintained component can destroy the other. And, conversely, a well-maintained die will increase the useful life of a stamping press as much as a well-maintained press will increase the useful service of a resident stamping die.

7.23 Assembly Tooling

7.23.1 Assembly equipment requires preventive maintenance, as much as any other component of the part-making process. How does tooling PM affect the assembly process? The answer is that PM eliminates variation.

7.23.2 Unless the assembly equipment is tightly controlled, the variations caused by normal wear and tear will make it virtually impossible to simply load and run a line without first readjusting clamps and fixtures to compensate for the damaged and failing components of the assembly process.

7.23.3 Without a comprehensive tooling PM program, every run of panels could be – and usually are – different from the previous run. Once again, assembly fixtures and clamps may need adjusting and "tweaking". As was mentioned before, even the proper use of press tonnage monitoring systems will have a positive affect on the assembly process.

7.23.4 Equipment that moves a panel from die operation to die operation is another candidate for preventive maintenance protection. Before this subject is discussed, one thing needs to be made clear: homemade end clamps and "fingers" are a waste of money. There can be no "maintenance" of a glob of weld and cold rolled steel. Very fine, fully adjustable and replaceable, component systems for robotic transfer as well as transfer bar systems are available and absolutely necessary if that transfer system is to become part of a world-class quick die change procedure.

7.24 Tooling PM

7.24.1 Tooling PM may be just one part of a total productive maintenance program. But, it is a prime component. And it is a component that has been largely ignored in the past. Maintenance PM Practitioners have had a hand in that criminal behavior. Tooling has just as much right to be maintained as equipment does.

7.24.2 The argument against tooling PM is that each tool is unique and collected data would not be relevant to any other tool. In their field, any 500 hp GE electric motor, for example, should perform as efficiently as any other 500 hp GE electric motor – and it should. Multiply that motor by the thousands that may be in service and the hundreds of thousands that were ever in service and there is an accumulation of data and history that can be used to qualify or rate any particular installation. This database will also allow the formation of a credible budget allocation for maintaining the equipment in question. Obviously, that's true.

7.24.3 Tooling PM may be different in the broad base of experience available. However, some similarities exist.

For example:
- Tooling for a particular part is very similar from year to year and model to model;
- Many components are standard items and have a performance history. Just ask the manufacturer for data.
- Repetition is inherent in the process as a tool attains thousands (or millions) of cycles during its useful life.
- Unique or not, periodic checks will uncover developing problems before they are serious enough to stop production.

7.25 PM Committee

7.25.1 A properly formed PM Committee should include representatives from many groups of specialists, based both in and out of the plant.

- First of all, the Coordinators should be selected from the ranks of the hourly trades and classifications. Coordinators will instinctively know what is needed to maintain tools, equipment, etc
- Either before or after that occurs, the PM Champion should be named. Ideally, the Champion will be at a superintendent level or higher since there will be a lot of "heavy-lifting" to do. They must be someone who can make things happen and also act as the Plant Manager's control mechanism.
- Someone from the I/S department would bring computer-based expertise to the table and can help ensure that proper software is available to support the PM Process
- A member of the supervisory staff can represent the foreman and general foreman and be the messenger who

will allow their counterparts to maintain integrity during the implementation phase.

- A management member will carry the message to the Plant Staff and ensure cooperation between departments as the PM procedure dictates.
- Facilities people will be able to anticipate changes to their equipment as each department implements their share of the PM Process. Additionally, they can provide fundamental support for the changing needs of each area of the plant.
- Advanced Manufacturing's member on the Committee can help direct the PM process and, in particular, steer the data collection efforts so as to capture the appropriate data that allows for continuous improvement of tooling designs and manufacturing procedures.
- The Controller must be a member so that, as they are manifest, there is an awareness of the financial benefits derived from the full implementation of a comprehensive PM program. Re-appropriating floor space (no longer used for part storage) should occur in a timely manner, as an example.

7.25.2 This may seem as overkill when it comes to committee size. However, politics is a major consideration in the successful adoption of any new process. Direct involvement in the primary committee responsible for that new process implementation will provide each participating area of the plant with first-hand information that directly affects their zone of responsibility.

7.25.3 A final issue concerning the "networking" theme is the sharing of data and technology between the various PM Coordinators throughout the plant. It can mean something as simple as sharing a checklist for the double-wheel tool grinder that exists in every area of the plant. It also means pooling resources to purchase infra-red cameras and ultra-sonic leak detectors that can be used by many departments during their normal PM activity.

7.25.4 In short, since they have a common goal and possess overlapping responsibilities, the various PM committee members need to work together because their particular department's fate is closely linked with the fate of every other department in the facility. The goal? Profitability! Every process must sell their product to the next process at a price that exceeds their particular process' cost. That cost takes a nosedive when quality, reliability and throughput are ensconced as primary objectives in any manufacturing enterprise.

7.25.5 Preventive maintenance is the first, and most important, step in the process of maximizing quality, reliability and throughput. Reliability Centered Maintenance comes next as select issues can be addressed. Resolving specific issues, through RCM, increases the opportunity to advance to Total Productive Maintenance (TPM). TPM becomes more of a reality as the entire manufacturing facility implements a comprehensive PM program. TPM is not something that happens in a week. It happens when processes become completely controlled.

7.25.6 Achieving such a lofty goal requires that the entire PM initiative is implemented in a systematic, continuous program that follows procedures that are mutually agreeable.

7.25.7 Once the overall procedures are established, the entire PM activity can then be provided to the rest of the PM crews through training or interactive workshops. These workshops can serve as extensions of the activities that identified the initial PM codes and checklists.

7.25.8 Sharing "new" technology is a mutually rewarding transaction. If turf wars are set aside and hourly trade people can freely interact, new uses for existing technology can provide significant benefits. For example: ultra-sonic leak detectors that are used to hunt down and eliminate air/gas leaks by the press maintenance crew, can be used in the die repair area to locate leaks in the gas springs mounted to the various dies and slides – eliminating hundreds of hours of applying "soap bubble" technology. Sharing information gathered from die maintenance records can assist the maintenance crew by indicating a developing problem on one of their presses due to worn gibs and such. Usually, the hourly people will have a good idea of how to use these tools to their greater benefit.

7.25.9 In line with this thinking, after the program collects and stores significant data, the use of common or shared databases will become an issue. Best idea is to encourage a shared use from the outset. Obviously, "read only" provisions can apply. However, the reporting functions must allow full access to both/all databases. Such sharing will enhance the ability to locate/identify developing problems caused by tooling that share the same equipment and machinery.

7.25.10 In multi-plant companies, the common processes can be refined much more quickly when each plant's experiences are shared with every other plant. This concept will be difficult to realize since plant rivalries can erect a higher barrier between physical entities than may be constructed within the environment of a single plant governed by the same management staff.

7.25.11 Industry conferences and local symposiums can provide a significant source of training for a PM coordinator as well as another place to give and get pertinent information that will help develop the plant's PM capability.

8. Why preventive maintenance?

These remaining chapters will serve a two-fold purpose: to summarize the case in favor of a comprehensive preventive maintenance program for tooling and detail the arguments against a tooling PM process, and to explore the rewards that can issue from such a program.

At the top of anyone's list, in favor of the implementation of a particular manufacturing process enhancement, must be a financial consideration. What monetary benefits can be realized and do they outweigh not only the dollar investment but also the impact of the aggravation index, which will temporarily increase whenever there is a change in a manufacturing process that has been used for years. Pure and simple, PM is a common sense approach. If oil changes make sense relative to an automobile's engine performance, then regular use of a check-listed maintenance procedure makes sense relative to the tooling used to make the automobile. Financial investment will be negligible if the approach is incremental. Start with a few tools, then the entire population of a production line assignment. By the time there is recognition of the ability to implement the program plant-wide; cost savings from the earlier steps will justify that implementation. This is not an equipment-based PM program. There are no electronics involved at the outset – save a computer to hold the data that are generated. Some electronics can be employed at a later time, but they will be used to bolster a maturing and successful process.

Second on the list should be the morale of the employees. A positive outlook regarding their employer, the safety of the workplace, continuing employment, and respect for their environment tends to encourage productivity and attention to the details of their job performance. That morale will be greatly enhanced if the input of hourly employees is sought and utilized from the outset. This is true whether there is a union presence in the facility or not. There are special considerations that must be recognized when there is a union present but, when discussing morale, all hourly employees, union or not, will react more positively when their input and guidance is actively solicited.

If a customer will pay handsomely for anything that is placed in a parts container, there is no need to consider quality. That customer is a deranged junk dealer. For any other customer, quality production defines their relationship with every manufacturer with which they do business. Quality does not occur unless it is actively pursued, and a commitment is made on the part of management and the comptroller's department to produce quality products. Goals, and the activities that pursue those goals, must be endorsed by management and become part of the supervisory staff's annual review criteria.

The price must be paid. It does no good to tear a tool apart only to find that parts and supplies, or time, are not available because of some mindless 10% cost-containment measure that some companies utilize on a regular basis. Many people tend to feel that there is always 10% "fat" in any operation and, to make matters worse, everyone and every department must suffer alike as the belts are tightened.

PM greatly reduces downtime and increases productivity. It saves money and provides the means to gain control of the stamping process. When the "fires" of failure are no longer raging out of control, a reasoned, focused approach to the stamping and maintenance process can be implemented. Manpower needs can be measured. As downtime is reduced and more tooling is needed to fill the presses, that can then be fully utilized, it is reasonable to expect that more tool and die makers will be needed, in addition to an increase in the number of press operators. Additional manpower needs can be determined by analyzing the sum of collected data to arrive at a "budget" of manpower and supplies. Manpower and supplies are necessary to support tooling of specific configuration, running through a particular stamping press, operated and maintained by the manufacturer.

Reliability and quality combine to produce salable throughput. That process is the essence of a successful stamping operation. Reliability is producing the same part to the same standards at each and every stroke of the press. Preventative Maintenance will deliver that reality. As it does, adjustments will be necessary within the manufacturing process. Manpower re-assignment will be a much-needed boon as press troubleshooters, or "fire-fighters", will not be needed in quantity as they were before a PM program was implemented.

However, before anyone gets relieved from their job, the fact that all presses can now run parts all day, every day, means that more opportunities exist for increased throughput. The newfound capability will affect job scheduling and encourage the addition of more part production. Reducing the cost to produce a product improves the manufacturer's ability to offer competitive prices and acquire additional work, which will enable the increased capacity to provide more income for the shareholders.

Another benefit to be realized from reliability and consistent quality is an increase in the number of profit centers. Whatever floor space was designated to part storage can now be utilized for other types of profitable activity: more production; additional services, such as sub-assembly and small quantity packaging; in-house die construction; and tool improvements that can further enhance quality and throughput of the manufacturing process.

Process optimization is what separates world-class manufacturers from fledgling, or failing, manufacturers. Fledgling and failing manufacturers are those who pick up the scraps when bargaining to fill their production capacity. The record keeping that should accompany the PM program will provide the data needed to identify the shortcomings of any tool. Process optimization begs the question: why does this tool, in this press, operate at less than the press manufacturer's stated cycles per minute, per hour? What improvements to the tooling, the transfer mechanism, or the material handling can be made to match press capability? The aforementioned record keeping also allows the identification of non-tooling related failures. If every tool that runs in a particular press, for example, experiences similar problems then it's possible that the press is the culprit and that further investigation is required. Or, possibly, adjustments to the press PM program are in order. Optimization applies to every aspect of the manufacturing process, including the

PM program. Use of data will lead the way to the next step in tooling and press maintenance: predictive maintenance.

Predictive Maintenance (PdM) makes it possible to anticipate pending failure through the use of electronic devices. There is a cost involved for the electronics and for the ongoing support by technicians. Support technicians will observe the flow of data that will indicate the need for a maintenance activity. In-die sensors track the change or deterioration of die components through the use of ultra-sonic stress waves. These ultra-sonic stress waves can be analyzed regularly to more closely predict tooling failure. The best news is that these systems can be married to the press monitoring system to transport the signal through existing fiber optics to a central monitoring area. In other words, the same people can monitor tonnage monitors, infrared sensors, and lubrication and die sensors with no increase in expense. The actual value of PdM will be determined by the perceived cost-savings to be gained from PdM that is not readily available through a comprehensive PM program. Again, the basis of the maintenance program is a comprehensive preventive maintenance program.

Most comptrollers would love to be able to accurately project a maintenance budget. The first step is to gather data for every instance of failure and maintenance for every individual tool in the plant. After that data collection has matured, average wear rates can be identified and assigned based on the complexity of a tool. An average trim die, for example, can be assigned a complexity rating of three, a simple trim die (small part, short trim edge) would be assigned a rating of one, and a complex trim die (quarter panel with overhead cams, collapsing post and 120 inches of trim) would be assigned a rating of five. Of course, any variation can fit easily within these standards, or a scale of ten-points can be used if desired. The point is to assign a complexity rating for every type of tool in the plant and then begin the process of computing the averages for die life, repair durability, maintenance performed and so forth. Since the cost per hour of basic operations as well as labor costs are known, then the average wear and tear on a type of tool is also known, and a budget can be easily constructed. If necessary, the maintenance budget can be refined as more experience with the PM program is gained.

DOWNTIME reduction is the main focus of any manufacturing operation. Quality is paramount given that a loss of quality will be considered a failure. When failures occur, the press is stopped and DOWNTIME begins to accumulate. Quality-control inspectors allow presses to operate and stamping strives to keep the presses operating. When tools and equipment are maintained on a consistent and regular basis, higher levels of production ensues. Unfortunately, too many manufacturers are content with process efficiency in the sixty percentile or less, and make up for this inefficiency by raising the price to secure and maintain a small profit. Eventually, the manufacturer will price themselves out of the market. They can go so far as to export their work to foreign countries where wages are low and inefficiency is masked by a lower cost.

Deciding that the stamping process can be improved, by utilization of a comprehensive tooling preventive maintenance program, will signal the employees that management is making an effort to keep their work in house, thereby ensuring their jobs. That support will be recognized and, usually, returned. However, the "we've been doing it this way for fifty years so it must be good" mentality has also affected the workforce. They may need time and constant reassurance that, this time, management intends to make real changes and is willing to listen to the suggestions of the trade-persons who do the actual work. The only thing more important, and more difficult, than changing work practices is changing attitudes.

The successful implementation of a comprehensive die PM program will depend on a significant change of attitude by all involved in the manufacturing process. An adjustment is necessary but extremely hard to achieve in many cases. Bogey-men have been concocted as fall-guys for every failure ever experienced by today's society. Workers in one plant demonize the workers in another, similar plant because they are compared to that other plant and found lacking. Foreigners "steal" their jobs and work for less money and benefits. "Scabs" are under the thumbs of their bosses and work too hard for their meager wages. Unions protect the lazy and incompetent and drive up the prices on their goods while producing inferior products. The excuses are legend and entirely bunk.

For the most part, workers expect to earn their wages by putting in a full day and doing what they can to enable the company to make a profit (from which they are paid, of course). Attitudes become "adjusted" when supervisors and managers try to impose changes without adequate preparation and analysis of the unintended consequences attendant to those changes. High-profile awards are conferred on those companies that make a top-to-bottom transformation in the attitudes and activities of their organization. Tooling PM does not require that level of change. But the determination to change attitudes is essential to success. Attitude will fill out the PM checklist or it will actually do the checking of the tool. Attitude will truthfully assign the actual hours of repair performed on a tool, or it will work a crossword puzzle instead. Exaggerations exist. This is not an exaggeration.

9. Why not preventive maintenance?

Earlier in this book, I suggested that the most accurate method for evaluating the success of a comprehensive PM program is to determine the cost of each square foot of plant space on Christmas Day. This means, the cost to the manufacturer, not including labor costs or material costs. The point is to rid the process of inflated estimates that damage the credibility of any proposal that asks for fundamental changes in the way business is conducted. Floor space utilized to store a surplus of parts, which provide leeway when trying to produce enough parts to meet production quotas, has a fixed cost which can be re-allocated to a profit-making enterprise. The reference is to a process that is considered seriously out of control. Actually, this is a misnomer. Any process can be deemed "in control".

The controls may include unlimited amounts of capital, everlasting overtime and around-the-clock operation, constant replacement and/or addition of machinery, habitual re-work and handling of manufactured parts, and a constantly shrinking profit margin. The ultimate control is reached when the plant is closed and the workforce is sent home because the bank account is empty and no one will purchase the over-priced, poorly manufactured products made by their company or unit plant.

After closing, the ulcers and other health problems caused by working in the pressurized atmosphere of a failing company will be paid by the individual. When the paychecks stop, so do the benefits like health care and retirement pensions. At this point, the "If Only"s begin.

If Only, every level of management had supported PM. Supervisory review criteria might have been adjusted to guarantee a full measure of support from supervisors. Work areas could have been altered to facilitate job flow and equipment could have been provided to speed up the maintenance process.

If Only weak managers had been properly motivated, or replaced, to inspire trust and cooperation from the workforce. So the transition from unplanned catastrophic failures to regular, planned maintenance tasks would have been methodical, reasonable and successful.

If Only union representatives had understood the implications of open hostility toward a change in the way their work is performed. They may have taken the time to understand that what they do will not change, just how they do it and why the records they keep will only improve their future with the company. A stable, cost-effective manufacturing process will help to ensure that there will be less of a transient workforce and more of a stable work environment with greater safety for union members and more profit to share with the company. In addition, by eliminating storage space and increasing workspace more of their sons and daughters can join them in the workforce. The workforce will enjoy a better than average standard of living as a result of their parent's cooperation with a reasonable approach to quality control, and the resulting increased throughput for the employer.

New management can negatively affect the continuing development of any process or proposed change. This is especially true concerning a concept that is new to the industry, such as PM for tooling. Almost everyone understands the value of equipment PM. Mostly, it requires controlling the environment in which the equipment operates. A GE motor, for example, is interchangeable with any other GE motor of like size and configuration. GE makes millions of motors and the same motor will run a pump for the petroleum industry or it will run a pump for an electrical-generating public utility. Performance specifications are abundant and such machines are easily compared with thousands of similar machines, with respect to performance. Recording and keeping data for comparison across the industry is easily accomplished. Since most tooling such as dies and fixtures are relatively unique, comparison is difficult. That means, there is very little to talk about in trade journals relative to tooling PM. Most of what is written is usually with regard to specialized industries that utilize hi-speed presses and progressive dies that have been constructed with more exotic metals. This comparison will involve the durability of carbide inserts v. oil-hardened steels, or some other new steel. Anyway, with so little written about tooling PM, do not expect the new manager to have much of a grasp of what is being done in the plant concerning tooling maintenance. And, if they are not familiar with the process, they, like the managers were prior to PM implementation, will be extremely skeptical of placing their future at the disposal of an unfamiliar maintenance procedure. On-going education is the key to understanding the necessity of a comprehensive PM program. Understanding and commitment should start at the top manager's office and continue on down to every existing employee, and future employee, who works within the manufacturing process.

Inspired and insistent leadership will be needed to overcome the misgivings of older management who have operated a particular way for twenty or thirty years. It is hard to argue with the fact that they have been successful for so many years doing what they do best: working with the system and meeting production standards no matter how long it takes and with little regard for how much it costs. The rule of thumb used to be that the customer is to be satisfied whatever it takes. In a world with little or no competition, this system will work because there is no more-efficient way to make the product. In the new world, there is plenty of competition based on quality as well as cost-efficiency. Efficiency in the range of 50 to 55 percent is no longer sustainable in today's marketplace. The intrinsic cost of such a system requires that higher prices must be levied in order to compensate for this method of manufacture. Obvious to most anyone, is that those who refuse to change their ways will become forcibly retired or they are awaiting a fast approaching voluntary retirement.

This situation is very unfortunate. Managers and supervisors have valuable skills and, most important, considerable experience in the manufacturing industry. They can help to provide a reasoned, gradual transition to total productive maintenance. They can aid the success of their employer and fellow workers and, in turn, strengthen their own retirement benefits, which are based on the vitality of the corporate entity. To borrow a seafaring analogy, they may view themselves as lighthouses. They are perched on stable ground and constantly warn of imminent danger. They should, more properly, be buoys that are sometimes moved in response to current conditions as they provide guidance to safe harbor.

An absentee manager can provide a challenge of a different sort. A subordinate, or unit, plant may be left to its own devices and simply provided with a budget and a production quota. There will be no interference from corporate level people unless costs rise and production quotas are not met. Except, of course, there will always be the annual "belt-tightening" exercises where all departments and levels of employment will feel an equal pressure to conform to the leaner and meaner standard of efficiency.

It is much easier to prepare for the "belt-tightening" than it is to cringe in fear and hope that the exercise will be dropped this year. A better plan is to begin a modest, but comprehensive, tooling PM program. Use the forms provided by reconstructing them on a software program such as MS Excel; establish rough estimates of cycle frequencies for PM checklist activities; select pilot areas for limited implementation; compile data as they are available and generated by trades people and production supervisors; expand and edit the process as it matures. These are very simple activities that will establish the basic criteria for program support while providing the financial justification for continued participation and expansion.

The strength of PM is that it is simply common sense put into action. If metal is supposed to move during the stamping activity, facilitate that movement by removal of galling and then polish the surface. If the die trims the part, check for chips and cracks and keep it sharpened. If there is punching involved, sharpen or replace the punch or button and keep the slug holes clear.

The weakness of PM is that it is common sense. Simple solutions are extremely suspect because there is always the thought that common-sense activities are being done already. In fact, they are rarely being done and, for sure, they are rarely recorded and the trends are hardly ever analyzed. In fact, the biggest bang-for-your-buck activity is washing the die/tool on a regular basis. The second? Keeping the press bed clean and clear of debris.

10. Rewards

Any discussion about controlling the stamping process, as part of the overall business of a manufacturer, must, out of necessity, include its affect on the *bottom line*. Although managers will find that there is minimal investment relative to beginning a tooling PM program, the fact is, that to be properly supported and to gain the maximum benefit from such a program, the entire stamping operation and material handling operations must also be improved and constantly maintained. Fortunately, the case for equipment PM has been made and is valid for any and all industries.

An entire sector of manufacturing is devoted to preventive and predictive maintenance techniques and electronics that help to maximize output and performance from presses, conveyors, stock feeders, rolling stock, environmental controls, etc. In addition, most of the supplier industries have increased their abilities to control the composition and consistency of sheet metals, cutting fluids, lubricants, drawing compounds, coatings, and other supplies. These refined and capable components insist that tooling be included in the PM program and be allowed to benefit from the rest of the process. The current industry even has a name for it, Total Productive Maintenance (TPM). TPM is the real culprit, and is aimed at "stealing" American jobs to be reassigned to cheaper foreign suppliers.

Many foreign suppliers are supported by their government, which is determined to establish a manufacturing base for their emerging economy. When little or no base exists, and government provides the funding, state of the art equipment, and the latest processes utilized to drive that nation's bid for economic vitality. Therefore the domestic manufacturing community is pitted against a state of the art business rival and is forced to compete with less than adequate equipment and no sense of process and/or maintenance control. Much like being in a narrow mountain pass with an adolescent enemy perched on higher ground. They can and will inflict terrific wounds, and yet they are still learning how to fire their weapons! In other words, there is still time, but that time is running out.

Why in the world do American manufacturers willingly transfer so many profit centers to foreign businesses? Are they hiding behind the skirt of their own inefficiencies? Cowardice? Corporate structure? Ultimately, management must accept the blame for the inefficiency of their factories; their lack of process control; and the expenditure of potential profit for out-sourced, manufactured goods. It is management that must regain control of the production process and foster a job-saving attitude amongst their hourly employees, while inspiring leadership within the ranks of their supervisory employees.

Morale is a critical component, which affects the efficient operation of any business. Even the cynical admit the role morale plays in a successful business when they say: "The beatings will continue until morale improves", a fitting acknowledgement of this vital psychological metric. Morale is directly affected by the looming possibility of job loss. Even talk of out-sourcing work causes wild speculation and rampant rumors to affect members of the workforce in a negative manner. A responsible manufacturer will be better served by researching methods to avoid the loss of a profit center. A profit center that has been built over the years, and one which has produced trained and experienced associates. These trained and experienced associates know that their livelihood depends on producing a quality product, at a reasonable cost, that provides an adequate wage and reasonable profits for the owners/stockholders. The method to improve and control the process is a PM program for the entire manufacturing process.

This entire book concerns itself, ultimately, with process control. There is little reason to expound on the benefits of eliminating the failures generated by an out-of-control manufacturing process. Virtually all of the stamping trade magazines present articles that deal with the various aspects of process control (PC). They include their charts and trending software results to document the validity of PC. Rather, this book has dealt with only one aspect –albeit a vital aspect – of the sheet metal stamping process: PM for tooling. While equipment PM has been widely documented, tooling PM is not. Each tool is somewhat unique and engineers may not be comfortable with reliance on a body of knowledge that began when a specific tool entered the stamping press for the first time. Be that as it may, there is great value received by actively pursuing that data and refining the PM program for that tool as it matures in the system.

There are so many similarities between the tools themselves and the operations they perform that financial justification can be found for support of a comprehensive tooling PM program. The steps provided in this book have been used with success at a major automobile manufacturing plant and achieved a multi-million dollar a year cost-avoidance dollar. In addition, the manufacturer developed repeatable quality and dependable throughput for every tool and, all tools were able to run at or near press capability for production. Tools included in the program produced, primarily, large automotive skin panels run in every type of press, including modern transfer presses as well as WWII era OBI presses. The die population included five and six station components run in older four posters as well as progressive dies run in state-of-the-art blanker presses.

Not every type of die has been part of the actual exercise. But, there is no reason to believe that any die would not benefit from being included in a comprehensive tooling PM program. The reader is invited to visit www.diepm.com and peruse the forms and documentation that are available on line.

Appendix

1. Current State Report Example
2. Die PM Repair Codes Example
3. Draw/Redraw Preventive Maintenance Checklist Example
4. Feedback Form Example
5. PM Workcell Layout
6. Standard Operating Procedure Checklist Example
7. Suggested Downtime Codes Example

All forms contained within this Appendix may be downloaded from the author's web site: www.diepm.com

Current State Report Example

Type	Measure	How Often	When?
Mean Time between Failure	Elapsed time between system failure caused by a die problem.	Monthly	Immediately
Mean Time to Repair	Elapsed time for repair to be accomplished in the die maintenance area – not in the press.	Daily	Immediately
How Many PMs	Simple count of actual PM procedures performed	Monthly	Immediately
Downtime	Average monthly downtime attributed to die failures.	Monthly	Immediately
Mean Time to Perform PM	Average time to perform a PM by die maker.	Daily	Immediately
PMs done/not done	Simple comparison of completed PMs v. scheduled PMs not done in expected time-frame	Monthly	Immediately
PM v. Repair	Inverse relationship between time spent repairing dies and time spent performing PMs	Monthly	Immediately
Resolved Complaints	Number of quality complaints v. resolved ones	Monthly	In a year
Manpower Allocation	Track movement of personnel resulting from increased reliability of stamping process.	Semi-annual	In 2 years
Quality Improvement	Comparison of number of quality complaints.	Semi-annual	In a year
Reliability	Failure free production runs – simple count	Monthly	Immediately
General Status	Periodic update for management review.	Semi-annual	Immediately

DIE PM REPAIR CODES (Example)

PRIMARY EQUIPMENT FUNCTION
1 TRIM DIE PROBLEM
2 FLANGE DIE PROBLEM
3 DRAW / REDRAW DIE PROBLEM
4 PIERCE DIE PROBLEM
5 PROGRESIVE DIE PROBLEM
6 TRANSFER DIE PROBLEM
7 MISC/ENGINEER ACTIVITY

EFFECT ON PARTS PRODUCED
01 AUTOMATION PROBLEM
02 BLANK/STEEL PROBLEM
03 BURRED OR TORN EDGE PROBLEM
04 CAM PROBLEM PROBLEM
05 CRACK & NECK PROBLEM
06 DIE SET PROBLEM

SPECIFIC SUB COMPONENT
027 MISSING/DAMAGED RUN NUMBER
028 NUT HEAD MALFUNCTION
029 OPEN BUTT/JOINT LINE BETWEEN STEELS
030 HOLDING SURFACE DOESN'T EXTEND TO WORK EDGE
031 POST/DIE SURFACE DETERIORATION
032 PROXIMITY SWITCH MALFUNCTION
033 ROUGH/SHARP SURFACE ON DIE
034 SHUT HEIGHT ERROR
035 SLUGGED FORM IN POST/DIE
036 SLUGS ON RING
037 SPRING FAILURE
038 TOO MUCH/LITTLE CLEARANCE BETWEEN UPER &LOWER
039 WORN BEAD/BLANK HOLDER SURFACE
040 WORN FLANGE STEEL RADII
041 WORN GUIDE PIN/BUSHINGS

Draw/Redraw Preventive Maintenance Check List

Die Number: _____ **Date:** _____

	Indicate cycle									
	Cycle Frequency	50000	100000	150000	200000	250000	300000	350000	400000	Description	Done?
	Punch/Bull Ring Mounting	15	15	15	15	15	15	15	15	Check/tighten screws	
	Wear Plates								300	Return to original sizes	
	Storage Cushions	5	5	5	5	5	5	5	5	Check and/or replace	
	Balance Blocks	7	7	7	7	7	7	7	7	Check and/or replace	
Information	Weight	1	1	1	1	1	1	1	1	Check for Legibility	
Tags	Nitro Pressure	1	1	1	1	1	1	1	1	Check for Legibility	
	Danger	1	1	1	1	1	1	1	1	Check for Legibility	
Guidance	Guide Pins								60	Check for wear, replace if nec.	
	Guide Bushings								20	Replace	

Die Preventive Maintenance
Feedback Form

To: Supervisor / Line Die Maker
From: Die Preventive Maintenance Area #1 Office

Date: _____

Line: _____   Part Name: _____

Part #: _____   Die #: _____

Was any die work necessary before part was submitted to inspection?

Please Check: ☐ No   ☐ Yes   *If Yes, explain:*

_____

_____

_____

_____

Was the first part submitted to inspection OK or Rejected?

Please check: ☐ OK   ☐ Rejected   *If Rejected, explain:*

_____

_____

_____

_____

Was there noticeable improvement to the panel as a result of the PM?

Please Check: ☐ No   ☐ Yes   *If No, explain:*

_____

_____

Person who filled out form: _____   Shift: _____

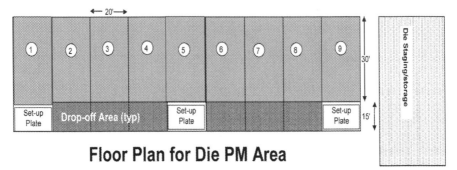

Floor Plan for Die PM Area

2 Reduced Size Cells and 7 Full Size Work Centers

Tool Box/Bench

Lower Die

Upper Die

Pad/Slide

Ready/ Waiting Die

Typical "Loaded" Cell

STANDARD OPERATING PROCEDURE

Type: Procedure	No:	Dept. No:

Title: **Trim/Pierce Die Preventive Maintenance Procedure**

Control O	Use of this procedure will enable the Die Preventive Maintenance Areas to warrant the tools that have been PdM'd as fit for service when returned to their production line.
Reason:	This procedure serves as a reminder to the die maker to check critical areas on the tools and repair/replace those areas that may be a problen during a production run.
Responsi	The die maker will perform this procedure before returning the tools to production and inform the die supervisor of any problem that requires scheduled release time to correct.

Procedure:

1) Remove all chipped or broken trim steels. Prepare properly and weld as needed.

2) Sharpen trim steels on the upper die. DO NOT RESHARPEN LOWER STEELS without re-establishing panel nest.

Suggested Downtime Codes Example

DESC:	DOWNTIME CODES		
DEPT.	**CODE**	**GROUP**	
		AUTOMATION	
Press	ACP	Cups	Any downtime associated with cups, adjusting, replacing, etc..
Press	APG	Destacker Pogos	Any downtime associated with pogos.
Press	AFM	Fanner Magnets	Any downtime associated with fanner magnets.
Press	ATV	Turnover	All turnover units
Press	AUN	Unloader	All items that cause problems with unloading parts from press
Press	ATO	Tryout	Scheduled release for automaton tryout.
Press	APL	Program Logic	Any modifications to automation programs.
		DIE REPAIR	
Press+Assm	DBU	Button/punch	All downtime associated with buttons, punch, run numbers,etc
Press+Assm	DGA	Gauging	Missing, broken, adjusting gauging.
Press+Assm	DLF	Lifter	Broken, loose, inoperative lifter systems
Press+Assm	DSS	Scrap shed	Anytime scrap build-up causes downtime
Press+Assm	DTO	Die tryout	Scheduled release for die tryout.
Press+Assm	DFS	Flange/trim/hem steels	Chipped, broken or worn steels.